The Night the Angels Cried:

A Mother's True Story

by

June Proctor

ISBN 0-9742483-0-4

Library of Congress Control #: 2003094803

Additional copies of this book are available by mail
for $9.95 plus tax and postage. Send order to:
June Proctor
Whispering Oaks Ranch
RR 4, Box 1193
Paris, TX 75462
(903) 785-0229

Printed in the U.S.A. by
Morris Publishing
3212 East Highway 30
Kearney, NE 68847
1-800-650-7888

This book is dedicated

to

my husband Richard

and

our daughters
Tanya and Sheilia

and

all our nieces and nephews
who pleaded,
"Aunt June, tell us what happened."

Acknowledgments

To my family and friends, pastors and chaplains, I owe a debt of gratitude beyond measure for inspiring me to share our story even when others said, "No one wants to read about death and dying." Neither did I until it happened to *my* family. Then I couldn't read enough books on how others resolved their grief after the funeral; how they left the grave side and reclaimed their lives when the world didn't stop, didn't care, didn't change, but their world *had* changed.

My fellow writers in the Red River Writers Club, Durant, Oklahoma, critiqued my early drafts of this narrative. My colleagues in the Oklahoma Writers' Federation, Inc. awarded the manuscript first place in the non-fiction book category. To these writers I am most thankful for their encouragement and pertinent advice.

The army family community reached across the nation and beyond its shores to comfort our family and call us back into action in the real world. I am proud of the chain of caring in the army command which responded to our needs and enabled us to move forward by sharing our burden of sorrow.

With my classmates in grief support groups also, I learned that "grief shared is grief divided." In the many layers of our human relationships lie precious diamonds in the rough, memories which are ours to polish and cherish long after death has silenced our loved ones.

To the staff at Morris Publishing I am most appreciative of their willingness to work with me to produce this publication for the benefit of the reader seeking to derive meaning, comfort, and purpose for one's life from the legacy of the beloved deceased.

Table of Contents

List of Photographs

Prologue

*"If I say, Surely the darkness shall cover me;
even the light shall be about me."*
- Psalm 139:11 KJV

"Honey, wake up. You're having a nightmare." I hear my husband's voice, feel his warm hand touching my shoulder.

"You're talking in your sleep again What were you dreaming?"

Intense emotion floods my brain. Tears flood my eyes. No words roll over my lips. There are simply no words to describe what I'm feeling. My heart pounds. My tongue is thick and dry.

"It's okay, honey. It was just a dream."

As the tears drain off, my breath returns with a sigh. "Thanks for waking me up," I whisper. "I'm okay now. Really, I'm fine." But I'm unable to tell him my dream. He nods and wraps me in his arms. He knows. He knows only too well.

The nightmares have left me speechless. I must reclaim my ability to put words to my feelings. I cannot go on like this. With pen in hand for the next year I write in my journal where my emotions safely struggle for release through verbal expression. It is my salvation.

The second year I review the insights uncovered by my journaling. On tear-stained pages I find renewed purpose for my life. Rolling a clean sheet of paper into my typewriter I start typing not knowing where my narrative will take me or when it will end.

One night to my astonishment I realize that I am nearing the resolution of my insufferable grief. A rising wave of exhilaration lifts me out of the waters of my tears and carries me down to the very last word of my story energized instead of depressed.

The grandfather clock in the hall chimes two in the morning. My husband is away at a stress management conference at Tucson, Arizona. A few hours later he phones at seven o'clock.

"Honey, the conference is great and a workshop for women is being offered this afternoon. How about driving over from Fort Huachuca this morning? It's only seventy miles and I know you would be glad you came."

Of course I would. Breezing along the wide open space of the desert highway a short time later in our Mercury station wagon I drink in the enchantment of the panoramic view of the desert dotted with red and yellow blooms on varieties of cacti. The early morning sun paints a backdrop of mountains in my favorite shades of lavender and blue. My solitary enjoyment comes to an end as I near my destination at Tucson.

After the first session of the workshop however I find myself out of sync with what we're learning. During the coffee break I chat with other women and realize I don't belong here today. I'm no longer properly stressed.

Slipping outside into the cool fresh air I walk a few steps, break into a jogging pace, and accelerate until I find myself sprinting, huffing and puffing, toward an imaginary finish line. I have not known energy like this since the day of the Accident.

I. What Happened?

(Christmas Eve, 1981)

The Christmas Portrait

"Children, obey your parents in all things; for this
is well pleasing unto the Lord."
                                    - Colossians 3:20 KJV

"Hey, Mom, what do you want for Christmas?" With that confident I-know-what-you-want look on his face, my eighteen-year-old son Terry Glen proudly rose from the overstuffed chair to his full height of six feet. Since he joined the army last January, he had relished the hero worship of his younger brothers and sisters.

"With you in the army and Mike away at college we haven't been able to take a picture of all you kids. Before the younger ones grow up and leave home, I would love to have a Christmas portrait of all my offspring," I proudly announced.

Earrings, cosmetics, or a box of chocolates always brought hugs and kisses form his mom in the past. This Christmas was different, however, and we both knew it. Terry Glen could be transferred overseas before next Christmas. I didn't say it, but I wanted him to have a picture of his brothers and sisters to carry in his wallet. Of course I needed one, too. We all needed one.

"Okay, Mom, if that's what you have your heart set on, then that's what you shall have. Trust me," he grinned. "I'll round up the little darlings." Saluting proudly he marched off like a drill sergeant to confront the troops.

"A picture?" asked nine-year-old Roger frowning. "That's all you want?" When I nodded, my youngest child shrugged his shoulders and mumbled something about choosing a tie. He hurried upstairs to the room he shared with his fourteen-year-old brother Ricky. Soon I heard the boys discussing their options.

"What are you going to wear, Ricky?"

"Well, I'm not going to wear a bow tie," Ricky laughed. "You've been looking for an excuse to wear that big one. You can wear it with the green corduroy vest Granny made for you."

Roger inherited a classy assortment of ties from his older brothers when sloppy clothes became the rage. He didn't care. With a bow tie he looked just like the rich bankers on TV. Fortunately the chaotic sixties and wild seventies had spent their energies. Roger was growing up on the cutting edge of self-improvement, not self-destruction. He liked the large gray bow tie with a pencil plaid of dark green.

"Dad bought me a navy blue suit with two pairs of pants," remarked Ricky. I listened to hear what Ricky would decide to wear, hoping I wouldn't have to argue him into the scarcely worn suit. The louvered doors squeaked loudly as he shoved open the closet and rattled the coat hangers.

"Hey, Man, I like the plaid pair."

I felt relieved. Plaid pants with the navy blue suit jacket would be an acceptable compromise. Better than his favorite worn out blue jeans.

"But I'm not going to wear a bow tie," he declared. "No way, little brother."

Ricky preferred shorts or jeans and T-shirts with outlandish slogans. He imitated everyone from chain-laden bikers to cowboys hobbling in Tony Lama high-heeled boots. Other days he looked like a stockbroker in a three-piece suit or a peace-nik wearing a headband, sandals, and beads. Our third son, fourth child, costumed himself in various roles as he searched for his own identity.

Toss in his allergies and hyperactivity, fueled by an insatiable curiosity, and the mix reaped a whirlwind of trouble for this bright little boy. He could be adorable or aggravating, cooperative or rebellious, involved or bored, but never still. In spite of his rambunctious nature, there was one person Ricky could always count on to anchor him. Tanya. Whenever he veered too far, his sixteen-year-old sister firmly steered him back into calmer waters.

Going into the kitchen to empty the dishwasher, I looked out the breakfast room window at the backyard patio shaded by a grove of live oak trees towering above the roof and shading the rock garden on the upper terrace. The whole family had worked hard to create a sense of a natural woodland. In the corner nook beneath the breakfast room windows, a waterfall splashed over layers of limestone into the goldfish pond, which the children had built with their dad. Over the edge of the pond the large shiny leaves of the banana tree waved in the gentle breeze.

Our twelve-year-old daughter Sheilia liked to climb up into the largest tree and read her favorite Phyllis Whitney mystery. When I was her age, I would climb out my second-story bedroom window to read my Nancy Drew mysteries perched under the gable above my window. I was glad Sheilia chose the oak tree instead of the roof for her special reading place.

Terry Glen knew where to find Sheilia. "Come on down, Ugly," I heard him teasing her. "Mom wants the gang to get a mug shot."

"I don't care if you call me Ugly. I look just like you." They both laughed at their private joke. Yes, they looked alike and with their captivating smiles and big brown eyes they also favored their glamorous Aunt Ruth. Uncle Ken and Aunt Ruth had no children of their own but they were the favorite aunt and uncle to nearly twenty nieces and nephews. People often thought Sheilia and Terry Glen were their children and they loved the ruse.

3

Reluctantly placing a worn bookmarker between the pages of *Listen for the Whisperer,* Sheilia climbed down the trunk of the gnarled old tree which served as her Swiss Family Robinson refuge. Before Swiss Family Robinson, before Phyllis Whitney, and after fairy tales, Huckleberry Finn tempted her just like he tempted Terry Glen at that age. Sheilia even built a raft down by the creek with her best friend Gigi Jordan. But Sheilia was no Huckleberry Finn. The raft sank. So did the next one and the next one. Sheilia discovered Phyllis Whitney's heroines just in time to awaken her own talent for sleuthing.

Sheilia came in and hurried upstairs to dress for the photo session. I followed with a stack of towels for the bathrooms across the hall from the girls' bedroom. I heard the girls discussing their brothers.

"You're not the only big sister. I'm a big sister, too," Sheilia announced. "Roger is *my* little brother. Ricky is *your* little brother."

Glancing into their room as I passed, I saw Tanya admiring herself in the double dresser mirror, while she brushed her long, chestnut brown hair. I wondered how she would respond to her younger sister's latest declaration of independence.

"Sounds fair to me," Tanya said. "You can play like you're a big sister, if you wish."

A good answer. No problem. After all, Sheilia had always been Tanya's Barbie doll. Tanya like to curl her hair, choose her clothes, tie her ribbons, and polish her fingernails. That is, until Sheilia became a seventh grader and turned into a pre-teen.

"I wish I was as pretty as you," Sheilia pined as she watched Tanya flit about in the soft blue and coral dress with its butterfly sleeves, empire waist, and tapering skirt. Tanya located her white heels and left the dresser mirror to Sheilia for her turn at primping.

The girls had been competing with each other for years to see whose hair would grow the longest. Aunt Ruth and I did the same when we were teenagers. I don't remember who won, but, as for the curliest hair, we both lost to our younger sister Joan. For years I let my hair grow below my shoulders until my first baby, Mikey, insisted on tangling his wee fingers in it.

"Maybe I should call myself Rapunzel," said Sheilia as she brushed her once golden hair which was turning brown lately. "That certainly sounds better than Ugly."

She looked at Tanya's shiny hair. "Forget it. You're the one who blossomed into a fairy princess ever since Mom let you wear lipstick."

Sheilia found another way to look older. The school teacher look. She dressed in a slate green skirt and color-coordinated print blouse. The cloth-covered belt looked trim with its smooth brass buckle.

"Since I'm Roger's big sister, I really should look like a teacher. It isn't every little brother who will wear a bow tie and act like a gentleman because his big sister says so."

Tanya slipped her narrow feet into her high heels. She didn't get to wear them often. But the heels were a must for the photo. Ricky and Sheilia were catching up with her in height.

When all of us assembled in the den a bit later, Tanya asked,"Am I always going to be this puny, Mom?"

"Honey, the word is 'petite.' You are NOT puny. Any girl who swims like a fish, rides horses and even a camel when we lived in Ethiopia, plays ball, and outruns the boys in track is NOT puny." Tanya smiled and stood taller.

Sheilia adjusted Roger's bow tie, then asked him if he liked her outfit. "Tanya thinks it's too plain."

"Looks fine to me," Roger replied after a once-over inspection.

Sheilia loved playing big sister to Roger and he appreciated the extra attention. Roger played sports. Football, soccer, and basketball. He opted out of baseball because it was too slow. Sheilia practiced shooting baskets with him on the backyard hoop.

She cheered when his team was winning and bolstered his spirits when they lost.

Roger repaid her. He listened to the stories she composed and acted out supporting roles when she rehearsed her lines for school plays. They were a good team.

"Hey, Tanya, you and I are all dressed up," grinned Ricky. "Won't Mom be surprised? You should see Terry Glen trying on Dad's sport coats."

"He doesn't need sport coats in the army," Tanya explained. "Seems funny he's as tall as Dad. Too bad Mike isn't."

Tanya sympathized with Mike. Although he was two years older than Terry Glen, the boys had been the same height since their early teens. Then Terry Glen outgrew Mike's hand-me-downs and Mike refused to wear Terry Glen's hand-me-downs. In Terry Glen's eyes, however, Mike was still ten feet tall. Mike feared the day when his brother might change his mind.

"Hi, everybody," Mike called from the doorway, announcing his arrival home from college. Terry Glen followed him inside from the front porch where he had been waiting for Mike to show up.

Looking up at Terry Glen, Mike joked, "Mom, I told you to stop feeding him. He's growing too tall."

"Son, the army is feeding him now and that's the way they like him."

The two boys had been like twins ever since Mike was nearly two years old. When my husband held young Mikey up to see our new baby, Mikey wasn't impressed.

"When is his mommy coming to take him home?" he asked.

"Mikey, this is your new baby brother," his dad explained. "His name is Terry Glen."

"Mikey's Terry?" He thought about it and decided to keep his baby brother in tow by teaching him a few things. Mike taught Terry Glen everything he knew, and Terry Glen added a few ideas of his own. What one of them didn't think of, the other one did.

Forever after they were inseparable even through all the stages of sibling rivalry. Before Terry Glen was three years old, Mike taught him to recite, *The Night Before Christmas.*

When he was eleven years old Mike saved his life in Heidelberg, Germany. We were returning to the United States from Kagnew Station in the province of Eritrea in Ethiopia where my husband had completed a two-year tour of duty at the U.S. Army Hospital. We spent a few days in Heidelberg with another army doctor's family. Our boys and his son ran down a forested slope. Terry Glen lost his balance and slammed into a tree.

As he lay on the ground, breathless and moaning, Mike knelt down and treated him for shock. Mike covered his brother with his own windbreaker, talked calmly to reassure him, and sent their friend for help. When the doctor arrived and took charge, he told Mike he probably saved his brother's life by not moving him. Later, when we learned of Terry Glen's internal injuries, we knew the doctor had been right.

Today Mikey's Terry still thought his older brother was ten feet tall in character. So what if he stood only five feet nine inches in his stocking feet.

When Mike enrolled at Southwest Texas State University in San Marcos, he worried that the girls were so tall. Where would he find a date his size? He didn't have to hunt anymore when the delightfully charming five-foot-one freshman Janice Kay Pecht enrolled. Somehow growing taller seemed less important–except when he saw Terry Glen again.

Mike stashed his luggage in his and Terry Glen's old room, checked his hair, and straightened his tie one more time. Then everyone climbed into our Volkswagen camper. As I drove to the mall to the Sears photography booth, I couldn't believe how well behaved my family appeared. Ricky began to have second thoughts about his choice of clothes.

"Mom, what will people think when they see us dressed like this?"

"They will think this is a good looking family," I promptly replied.

Smiles spread briefly across shiny faces and vanished as we pulled into the huge Sears parking lot. We disembarked and hurried through the mall before anyone recognized us. No one looked at us with raised eyebrows. That is, no one until we reached the studio.

"Oh, dear." The photographer had a dilemma. "When you said, 'children,' I thought they would be smaller." Apparently, I neglected to mention that the children ranged from nine years to twenty years of age.

"I'm not sure we can get them all into the picture," he said, shaking his head.

Our family crowded into the small space before the photographer's camera set-up. Not to be thwarted after successfully coercing all my children into decent looking clothing at the same time, I looked around for a solution. I knew we could do it. I insisted we do it.

The small room did not allow much space between the camera and the backdrop. Ah ha! The corner. We could use the corner to our advantage.

With the help of a chair and a small box behind it, the problem was solved. I asked Terry Glen to sit in the chair since he was the tallest. Mike stepped upon the box behind him. Along the wall on Mike's right Tanya stood on the floor next to Ricky. On Mike's left Sheilia stood beside Roger. Perfect!

Terry Glen sat in his favorite position, the center of attention. Mike towered above him and all the others. Tanya, poised in her high heels, stood taller than Sheilia and Ricky. Sheilia, having no need of a box or heels, stood taller than little brother Roger. Standing proudly by Terry Glen's side, Roger squared his shoulders like his hero and looked at the camera.

That was five years ago. Today was Christmas Eve. A few hours ago Roger died with his hero.

Seated: Terry Glen. Standing, *left to right:* Ricky,
Tanya, Mike, Sheilia, Roger. December, 1976.
      (Courtesy of Sears Studio)

Where Are My Children?

"In Rama was there a voice heard, lamentation, and weeping, and great mourning, Rachel weeping for her children, and would not be comforted, because they are not."
- Matthew 2:18 KJV

Gray skies, warmly lit homes, and snow-covered fields. The Maryland countryside resembled the Currier and Ives paintings on our Christmas cards. Maybe that's why it stayed locked in my memory. If I could hold on to that last scene, the two-story farmhouse with the pitched roof, I could stop the clock, stop the vehicle careening toward us, and rewrite the ending to that fateful day, Christmas Eve, 1981.

As I drove my family to Westminster, Maryland, from our ranch style home in Clarksburg, I felt blessed to have my grandchildren and four of our six children with me. We anticipated a full house tonight at Westminster United Methodist Church for the "Journey to Bethlehem" living scenes which all the Sunday School classes had been preparing. The Young Adult Class had invited Tanya to bring Ruth Ann and play the role of Mary with the baby Jesus. Terry Glen agreed to portray Joseph. The children's choir, which I directed, would be dressed like shepherds, singing and leading the procession through the halls to each event. Westminster had been our church home only since October when I accepted the position of religious education director.

Tanya was a bride when we left her behind in Norfolk, Virginia, three years ago. At that time Sheilia, Roger, and I accompanied my husband to Stuttgart, West Germany, where he would serve as Corps Surgeon at Kelley Barracks, the U.S. Army VII Corps Headquarters. When we returned to the States last summer Tanya was a single mother with two babies and a third one on the way.

I was with her when she gave birth to baby Ruth Ann by Caesarean section shortly before Thanksgiving. Three-year-old Becky told me to bring her mommy home from the hospital, "and don't forget the baby." Eighteen-month-old Paula, however, wasn't as pleased to share her mommy with a baby sister.

Terry Glen, home from his five-year stint in the army, rode beside me in the front passenger seat of our new Volkswagen Rabbit station wagon as we traveled over the hills of the Maryland countryside. Sheilia and Roger, now students at Damascus High School, rode with Tanya and her three babies in the back seat.

Since Maryland had not passed infant and child restraint safety laws at that time, Tanya held Ruth Ann in her arms. Becky sat on Roger's lap so she could look out the window with him at the snow banked along the side of the road. Sitting between Tanya and Roger, Sheilia tried to hold onto Paula who twisted and turned to see everyone and everything like her Uncle Ricky did when he was a toddler.

My husband was on duty at the Uniformed Services University of Health Sciences in Bethesda, Maryland, tonight. As professor of military medicine and commandant of students he worked overtime to provide the best possible instruction to the young medical students who would be commissioned as second lieutenants upon their graduation.

Suddenly a vehicle drifted across the center stripe. Bearing down on my horn I yelled. "What's he doing in my lane?" The driver was headed toward my right. If he didn't hit us first he would miss the curve and end up in the field. To my left I saw nothing coming and open frontage. Escape? The gap closed. Tires screeched. Metal crashed into metal. Glass shattered like chunks of ice.

I never felt the impact which slammed my head against the mirror and sent me back against the door jamb fracturing the base of my skull. When excruciating pain jerked me into consciousness I was stretched out on a litter on the ground. A warm blanket covered my shivering body. My clenched jaws steadied my chattering teeth. Out of the semi-conscious darkness I heard a woman's voice. My eyes made out a woman in a dark uniform leaning over my face.

"What happened?" I asked. She must be a rescue worker. She would know.

"You have been in a terrible accident."

"Where are my children?" I heard sounds of voices in the background.

"She's asking about her children." I strained to hear an answer among the confusion of noise.

"They're being taken to other hospitals," the woman replied when she leaned over me again. "You have a daughter named Tanya?"

"Yes. . . ." I held my breath.

"She's here with you."

I thought I heard her voice. Only a word or two, but Tanya sounded calm and far away. She wasn't crying or moaning. The children must be okay.

"We're going to put you on a helicopter to take you to the hospital. Tanya will go with you."

A terrific spasm gripped my right hip. I pressed down firmly with my hand trying to stop the contraction. "Please, I need a muscle relaxant." The intense agony shoved me down into unconsciousness again.

When I revived I was on a hospital examining table. Bright lights blinded me. Someone was turning my ankle. Pain shot up my leg to my hip.

"Stop! Please, stop!" I cried out. Whoever was torturing my leg did not stop. "Stop that!" I demanded and bolted upright.

A man apologized. "We thought you might have a broken hip. We were checking for range of motion." At that moment I knew my range of motion was going to be wider than he expected, if he twisted my foot again. To my relief he didn't inflict more pain.

Then I thought I recognized Tanya's voice. My blurred vision identified no one I knew. *Where is she? Why isn't she talking to me?* I heard her speaking in measured tones to someone else. *I must not embarrass her with anymore outbursts. At least she's here.* Hope flickered as consciousness slipped away once more.

I awoke in a curtained stall and a nurse told me I was in the intensive care unit. My body felt heavy as though I were buried under earthquake rubble. Every muscle in my being throbbed with pain. My ribs ached when I tried to talk. Breathing hurt. I asked for Tanya. The nurse assured me I would be able to see her, but said no more. For the first time I was afraid, really frightened. No one had mentioned Sheilia or the babies, nor whether Terry and Roger were with them.

What happened? How did we end up here? In a hospital? That car . . . in my lane. I honked. Why didn't he get out of my lane? The curve . . . snow . . . trees.

Oh, the pain. Why doesn't it stop? Can't they give me a shot or something?

Where are the babies? Dear God, please, don't let them hurt like this. Please, give them kind nurses who love little ones. Bring them safely to their mommy.

13

Does Richard know yet? The shock. How will he bear it? What can I say to him? I feel so helpless. Must get this pain under control.

As these thoughts whirled around in my head, I heard someone pull back the curtain. Opening my eyes I saw Richard. *Why is he wearing surgical garb? I'm not in surgery, am I?*

"Honey, I love you," Richard said softly as he swallowed hard. His face didn't show the shock, he later told me he felt, when he saw my badly bruised face. I couldn't move. Indiscriminate pain raged throughout my body like one massive wound. He kissed me gently and brushed my hair back from my forehead.

"You must get well for me and the girls. We need you."

"I knew you'd say that." I had counted on it. "Of course I'll get well." I tried to sound confident. "But Richard, what happened?"

"The man was drunk. You didn't stand a chance."

"Drunk? In the middle of the afternoon? I never thought of that. I wondered if he was drugged, however, because he didn't respond to my honking."

Richard had more to tell me. As an army physician he had been the one to break tragic news to families before. But nothing could have prepared him for this. The medical staff informed him that his wife and daughter knew nothing about the deaths yet. They said they thought it best to wait until he arrived, to tell us. Without hesitation he proceeded to give me a full report.

"Sheilia is at Westminster in the Carroll County Hospital. It was her doctor who notified me that you and Tanya were here. Tanya's still in surgery. I haven't seen her yet, but they promised to let me be with her just as soon as they take her to recovery. That's why I'm wearing this green surgical outfit."

"The babies," I said. "Have you seen the babies?" Richard slipped his strong hand under mine so that my hand rested comfortably on his. Then he answered.

"Honey, we lost them." The grief in his face undoubtedly mirrored my own.

"Oh, Richard," I gasped. "Poor Tanya. I didn't expect anyone to die." *Becky, Paula, Ruth Ann, how can we live without you? How can your poor mommy survive?*

"What about the boys?" My thoughts raced on. *Are Terry's legs broken? He's so tall and our VW Rabbit station wagon is so small. Roger's shoulders . . . will he be able to play basketball?*

Carefully, Richard laid his other hand over mine. "Honey, we lost them, too." His eyes were rimmed with tears now and his steady voice weakened. I wanted to hug him but I was unable to move without experiencing deep pain. We didn't know yet the extent of my injuries. All he could do for me was to touch me, hold my hand in his, kiss me on the forehead.

"Richard, oh, Richard," I sobbed, trembling like the aftershock of an earthquake (*why do I keep thinking of earthquakes?*) that had ripped our family apart, swallowing up our sons and grand babies. I wanted to hold onto my husband so nothing could take him from me, too. I wanted to wake up from this terrifying nightmare.

"I thought—we were going—to escape." My jerky sentences were punctuated by spasms in my hip. "It all happened so fast." My lip quivered as I recalled the vehicle coming toward me. "He headed—toward my right. I had—to go left. There was an open area."

By now I couldn't stop sobbing but I kept on trying to talk. "I thought—if we could make it—off that shoulder, at least—we would be ALIVE! I didn't expect anyone to die."

Tears trickled down Richard's face as he listened to me . I felt terribly hot. He rubbed the perspiration from my forehead.

"Sheilia . . . is she . . .?"

"She's going to be okay. Her injuries weren't as serious as yours and Tanya's. That's why they brought both of you here to the shock trauma unit."

A fresh flood of tears blinded my eyes at the thought of Sheilia lying all alone in another hospital without any member of her family with her to comfort her.

"Richard, go to Sheilia. She doesn't need to be by herself at a time like this."

But Sheilia was not alone. Independently of each other, Tanya and Sheilia had thought to tell the rescuers to phone the church. Richard learned from the hospital staff at Carroll County Hospital that our assistant minister, Reverend Ruth Ross, had gone immediately to the emergency room to be with Sheilia when the call came in. Our senior minister, Reverend Loren Gisselbeck, would drive to Baltimore to be with Richard, Tanya, and me at the shock trauma unit in the University of Maryland hospital. A clergy intern, Laura Lee Wilson, who knew her away around in our hospital, came with him.

Loren told Richard that lay persons had been called to lead the six o'clock worship service. My assistant, Kristy Bair, had pressed volunteers into service for the nativity scene, and gently advised the choir children that she would be replacing Mrs. Proctor as their choir director tonight. I had left gifts of small round tins of fruit flavored candy with a personalized Christmas card for each child in my office. I hoped Kristy remembered.

The ministers stayed with Richard until time to return to the church to conduct the midnight worship service scheduled to begin at 11:00 p.m. At Carroll County Hospital Ruth Ross left after promising Sheilia that she would check in on her again after the church service.

I had no concept of day or night or the hours passing quickly for me but glacially slow for Richard. He left my room to visit Tanya again after the nurse gave me something for pain. Overwhelmed by our incredible loss, I fell back into that darkness where no emotion penetrates and no fears intrude. I didn't know how long it was before Richard returned.

His sunken eyes and hollow cheeks told me he had not slept or eaten since he reached the hospital. "Pray for Tanya," he said. "I talked to the orthopedic surgeon." Richard took a deep breath and stood straight as though he was about to present a morning report on a patient he had worked up.

"Tanya suffered internal injuries to her liver, a collapsed lung, broken ribs, and fractured pelvis. Both arms are in casts. The right side of her body took the worst impact. Her right arm was crushed. They had to put in a steel plate. Her right kneecap was flipped open and her leg is now in a cast. Her little finger on her left hand was broken and the bones crushed along the left side of her hand."

He looked down mumbling, "She's not out of the woods yet." Both of us were crying.

"Richard, we can't lose her. She WILL hang on." At that moment I knew my job was to live for Tanya and to give her hope. Dying was not my job and it must not be her job either. We couldn't help those who had been killed. But those of us who survived had been saved for some purpose we did not yet know. For that reason we must bond together and not allow ourselves to be helpless victims the rest of our lives.

Richard said when he entered the recovery room all he could see were our daughter's wet green eyes and the tips of her fingers. She was hooked up to tubes. An oxygen mask covered her nose. Her fingers protruded from the casts on her arms and her right leg was in traction.

No one had told her that her babies were dead. Richard warned the nurses to be prepared. He must tell his daughter the worst news a young mother can hear, and at the same time give her the will to live.

"I told her we loved her and needed her to hang in there," he related the scene to me. "She wiggled two fingers and I thought she was asking about her brothers. She nodded and I told her we lost them. Then she wiggled three fingers and I knew she was asking

17

about her babies. Patting her fingers I told her we lost them, too, but we needed her to hang on for us. She nodded again and tried to say something but couldn't because of the oxygen mask."

Unable to pray without choking up, we closed our eyes in silence. God looks on the heart and our hearts were split wide open. Somehow the dark night slipped away into daylight. Cherished memories glimmered as I opened my eyes and closed them again to hold on to those visions of last Sunday when I played the piano for Becky's class.

Tanya, costumed like Mary in a peasant dress and shawl over her head, sat on a bale of hay cuddling Ruth Ann in her arms like the baby Jesus. Becky's class paraded around them singing, "Away in a Manger." Becky peered over her baby sister's blanket for a closer look, then smiled at her mother before joining the other children at the Christmas tree to hang the decorations they had made. It was the last Sunday in Advent.

Two weeks earlier Tanya's children were baptized with water from the Jordan River which Sheilia had brought back from Israel when she was baptized in the Jordan last spring. Tanya had been baptized as a teenager in Texas but as a single mother she chose infant baptism for her children. "I need all the help I can get," she had explained to Sheilia when she made her decision.

That Sunday morning Richard and I stood with Tanya at the altar, each of us holding a granddaughter while Ruth Ann lay sleeping on Tanya's shoulder. Reverend Gisselbeck gently lifted Becky from Richard's arms and baptized her first, sprinkling a few drops of water from the baptismal font on her blonde hair. When he handed her back to Richard after the prayer Becky reached out her arms to her granddad and to his surprise she planted a spontaneous kiss on his cheek. He hugged her and returned the kiss.

Paula however wasn't too sure she wanted any of this water stuff. She frowned, turned to Becky for support, and allowed Reverend Gisselbeck to gather her up, ruffles and all, from my arms. When he sprinkled the water on her hair, she leaned back and looked up. As he laid his hand on her head to pray, Paula wiped the water from her bouncy brown curls and frowned at me. She was still frowning when he handed her back to me.

Reverend Ruth Ross baptized Ruth Ann noting that she and the baby shared the same biblical name. Then she carried our tiny grandbaby up the aisle to show the congregation their newest charge whom they had promised to help rear in the Christian faith.
Becky looked concerned when Reverend Ross walked off with her little sister and strained to see above her granddad's head where she was going. Everything was okay when the minister turned around and came back to Tanya placing a quiet Ruth Ann in her mother's arms.

In her short life Ruth Ann portrayed the baby Jesus who represented the hope of the world, yet three days later our hopes for her life were extinguished when she suffered a violent death, as did our Lord. To me it was no coincidence that Ruth Ann was baptized with water from the same river where Jesus was baptized. These thoughts comforted me. I wondered if they comforted Tanya. In the Gospel of Luke 2:19 (KJV) the scripture reads, "But Mary kept all these things, and pondered them in her heart." Tanya had a great deal to ponder of both joy and grief.

When I awoke, the nurse brought my breakfast tray and informed me of Tanya's progress. I told her to tell my daughter that I was okay and that I loved her very much. That I would come to her room as soon as I could commandeer a wheelchair.

She smiled. "Tanya loves you, too."

Love bound our wounded family together this Christmas day. The apostle Paul wrote that "Love hopeth all things, endureth all things." (I Corinthians 13:7). By God's grace we would endure.

Left to right: Two and a half year-old Rebecca
(Becky) Anne Jeanette and one-year-old Pauline
(Paula) Marie Jeanette. May, 1981.

Tanya Marie (Proctor) Jeanette with her baby Ruth
Ann Jeanette in the roles of Mary and baby Jesus
at Westminster, Maryland, December, 1981.
(Courtesy of photographer Steve Shipley)

$\diamond$ 3

Homesick

"My heart is sore pained within me: and the terrors of death
are fallen upon me. . . . And I said, Oh that I had wings like
a dove! For then would I fly away, and be at rest."
- Psalm 55: 4-6 KJV

R-r-ring. R-r-ring. R-r-ring. My mind reaches for the phone
but my body does not respond. I haven't yet been able to reach
beyond my call button.

Please, someone. Answer my phone. It could be Sheilia.
Bearing down on my call button with my thumb, I'm relieved to see
a nurse rush in and grab the phone before it stops ringing.

"Hello." She smiles at me as she listens.

"Yes, she's here. Would you like to talk to her?"
Placing the receiver against my ear on my pillow, the nurse says,
"It's your mother."

Mother? A lifetime of memories rush into my mind. Terry
Glen was her favorite grandson. We usually called him by both
names to distinguish him from his Uncle Terry, Richard's brother
in Houston. Mother called him Terry Boy. *Lord, help me. What
can I say?*

"Martha June? Honey, I . . . we. . . uh, uh."

Please, Mother. Don't break down. I can't handle my shock and yours, too. Not yet.

"I'm going to be okay, Mother. The doctors and nurses are very good here and everyone is so kind." My voice sounds strange to me, as though I'm under water.

"Your sisters are here." Mother speaks clearly now that she has heard my voice.

I knew that my sisters Ruth and Joan would be at Mother's for Christmas. Joan's four children are the approximate ages of our four younger ones. I remember the year we gave our boys the Lionel train set. Richard and Joan's husband Max played with the train so much on Christmas Eve after the children were asleep that it didn't work the next morning. They had to make some adjustments.

Suddenly my body jerks as the cruel thought hits me that my own grandchildren's gifts lie under our tree at home. Becky and Paula will never play with their new dolls. Ruth Ann will never celebrate a first Christmas.

"Honey, I didn't know they would let me speak to you," Mother was saying. "Ken said that Richard phoned him and Ruth last night and promised to call us this morning. But we haven't heard anything."

"Richard's gone to the airport to pick up Terry and Linda," I explain. "They were in Tulsa with his folks when Richard called them." *I think that's what he said.* Fragments of his words circulate in my brain. Salty tears burn my eyes.

Richard needs his brother and sister. He can't go home to an empty house. Not on Christmas.

"Your father has been worried sick. I just couldn't stand it any longer, so Ken said we should phone the hospital."

I can't stand it any longer either, Mother. A sense of emptiness comes over me. All my feeble energy is consumed. *Yet I must handle these deaths for Richard's sake, for Tanya, and for*

23

Sheilia. "I'll tell Richard you called. The nurse needs to do some things for me now."

The nurse understands my signal and takes the receiver from my ear. She gracefully concludes the conversation with Mother, then writes some notes on my chart. We talk. Small talk. Nothing I need to remember. It doesn't matter. I want to wake up from this nightmare. I want to hold my grand babies.

Richard and his brother Terry walk in sometime later. I notice that Terry's eyes are bloodshot. "Linda's running a fever so we left her at the house," Terry says. I feel sorry for Linda, alone in our home at Clarksburg. The children's clothing was left strewn where Tanya sorted it when she dressed her children for the trip to Westminster. Linda will probably sleep in Tanya's room to feel near Tanya and her babies, if she sleeps at all. Linda is a lot like me in that respect.

"We've been to Carroll County hospital to visit Sheilia," Richard says. "Tomorrow she'll be coming home now that Aunt Linda's here. With both her arms in casts Sheilia needs help to dress."

I love you, Linda. Take care of my little girl for me.

Sheilia will miss the children. She spent a great deal of time playing with Becky and Paula after Ruth Ann was born so Tanya could care for her baby. She had a lot of experience from working at the Kelley Barracks post nursery in Germany where she was the assistant dance instructor for the pre-school and kindergarten children. When we went to Italy on vacation she talked about her young dancers the entire trip as though they were her own children.

Richard tells me the x-rays showed that Sheilia suffered a pelvic fracture. "She's getting around painfully, but she will be okay," he says. 'Fortunately she didn't suffer internal injuries like Tanya did."

I wonder if Sheilia will be able to dance again. Last year she convinced Roger that he was needed as a stage hand for the school play *Brigadoon*. In the production she danced and swayed collapsing on the chest of her lover who had been killed in a feudal altercation. Roger was so disturbed by the grief she portrayed that he couldn't bear to watch her dance the night of the performance.

"Martha June, I think we need to take some photos of you, if you don't mind," Terry says as he lifts his camera. A Houston lawyer, Terry sets aside his personal grief to prepare for possible legal ramifications.

"I'm not interested in any lawsuit, Terry. I just want to get home to my family." We have insurance and so does the other driver. Nothing more is necessary as far as I'm concerned. Just pay the bills and get on with living as a family again. Richard agrees with me about lawsuits, but thinks the photos should be taken anyway. I suppose he is right.

"Sheilia had visitors from the high school today, a couple of boys," Richard smiles. "They put a small Christmas tree on her bed stand. I think the boys knew Roger, too."

Richard said that Mable Price, a member of our church, brought a set of Trouble Dolls to Sheilia. The painted dolls from Russia were crafted as little containers of graduated sizes which fit inside each other to look like one doll.

"Mable told Sheilia she could tell her troubles to a Trouble Doll and put it under her pillow. While she sleeps the doll will handle her worries. It's a charming story, the kind Sheilia likes."

God bless you, Mabel.

Terry and Linda weren't the only ones Richard picked up at Dulles airport. Tanya's ex-husband, Bob Jeanette, was there too, in response to Richard's phone call to Bob's parents in Alabama.

"Bob's with Tanya now," Richard said. "They will need each other to work out their grief over their children."

Finally, Richard said that Terry and Linda had accompanied him to Mount Airy to identify the bodies of our sons and Tanya's children. At least he didn't have to do this alone. Ruth Ann's body hadn't arrived yet from Johns Hopkins hospital where she had been flown when her sisters were taken to Carroll County hospital.

25

At first I thought Richard saw how handsome Terry Glen looked in his new brown suit. Richard's face fell. "I didn't see the suit. The bodies were covered with sheets. The boys had to be examined for cause of death."

Terry Glen bought the suit just a few days before Christmas when Richard and the boys went shopping at the mall. Sheilia had wanted to go until Richard said the guys needed a night out together. Put that way, she understood. Actually they wanted to surprise us with the gifts they bought.

Thank you, Lord, for giving Richard that last special time with his sons. Why didn't I take a photo of them that night? Why didn't I take a picture before we left home for Westminster?

"I kissed the boys good-by for you and again for me," Richard said softly. "I kissed Becky and Paula for their mommy, too."

I can't imagine the morgue room. I don't want to. I feel a strange sensation when my eyes notice the rails on my bed, the white sheet covering my body, the flat pillow under my head, lying there motionless . . . hot tears dribble down into my ears assuring me that I'm alive– but my sons and the grand babies are dead.

The day has been too long. I close my eyes and bang on heaven's doors. *You made a mistake! You took my children! You took my grandchildren! How could you do that? I want them back!*

Richard reaches over the railing and squeezes my hand. "We need to get home and check on Linda. I'll phone your mother from home."

I learned later from Linda that he was unable to call Mother that night. Two reporters from the *Baltimore Sun* were waiting for him when he got home. They insisted that he take them down to Terry Glen's and Roger's basement bedroom. When I listened to the tape, some weeks later, I heard the hesitation in Richard's voice. "I don't think I'm ready for this."

But he acquiesced and entered our sons' room anyway. How could reporters be so cruel, so insensitive to a man's grief? Linda told me that because Richard was strong, she and Terry were strong.

From the moment I heard of this selfish intrusion into the privacy of our sons' room and my husband's personal grief I promised myself that I would never cry for the media. I was thankful that Richard's brother and sister had been present for Richard's sake.

Our home at Clarksville, Maryland, the day we purchased it, June, 1981. The new Volkswagen station wagon is parked in the driveway.

✦ 4

God's Mysterious Ways

"Heal me, O Lord, and I shall be healed."
- Jeremiah 17:14 KJV

Shadows beckon me to sleep. But whether awake or lost in nothingness I don't dream. Death must be like that. Nothingness. It's scary. I try to stay awake in the the curtained space of my hospital bed as the hours pass.

Beyond those curtains lie three more patients. I saw them when my curtain was open. All men. *Wouldn't Mother have a fit?* Not to worry. In our conditions gender is irrelevant. We're all helpless, more or less, or we wouldn't be in ICU. Are they hurting? Are they afraid? Must pray the fear out of this room.

Yea, though I walk through the valley of the shadow of death, I shall fear no evil. . . . (Psalms 23).

Fear is worse than pain. I'm afraid to think of never seeing Terry Glen and Roger again. I feel homesick, like when I went away to college at Oklahoma City University. When the first bitter cold spell swept through the girls' dorm, I wanted to go home to McAlester. I wanted to curl up in a blanket before the fireplace, drink hot chocolate with my family, and tell them about my new boyfriend, Richard Proctor.

I want to drink hot chocolate again with Terry Glen and Roger and promise them we will heal together. We will–in my journal. Terry Glen, you wanted to be a writer. You said when you

28

had lived enough adventure, you would write fiction. Then you joined the army. Mike taught you to read before you started to kindergarten. I checked out ten library books at a time for you in first grade. You read all of them before we got home. I was almost mad at you. Can you believe that? I would return to the library the next day and check out ten more books, with baby Sheilia in my arms and Tanya chasing Ricky through the stacks trying to drag him back to us.

You enrolled in a speed reading class in middle school so you could read more books by reading even faster. The teacher said you read so fast you discouraged the other students. He dismissed you from the course the second week.

I can see you reading now in that great library in the sky, Heinlein, Asimov, and all the best science fiction ever published. All the fascinating spy novels, mysteries, and intrigues, especially Shakespeare's plays and Greek mythology. Why only last week you were reading Homer's *Odyssey* for the umpteenth time. Now you have all eternity to read every book ever written. That's paradise, isn't it, son? No eye strain, no deadlines, no dead . . . .

A nurse pulls back my curtains. After checking my vital signs and asking a few questions, she dims the lights and leaves.

"I'm sorry, ma'am, to be here." The shaky voice comes from a man in the next bed. "I told them I was okay, but they brought me here anyway."

Why is he apologizing? Maybe he's chagrined at sharing a room with a woman. I turn my head and see an elderly man lying on the sheets, still dressed in street clothes and a dark overcoat. Somehow I never noticed when they brought him in. He stares at the ceiling tiles through thick lenses in his dark framed glasses.

"They need us where they can watch us," I say. "I'm glad for that. If you're okay, you'll be released soon, I'm sure." My voice resonates inside my skull like in a cave. Am I talking loudly? Fluid drains from my left ear and I slowly move my hand to my face to press the cotton back into my ear.

We talk about our accidents. His was a fender bender. It helps to talk; helps both of us I think. He sighs and speaks more comfortably the longer we talk–like a grandfather, philosophically. Like the grandfather I never knew.

A young black man stirs in the bed against the wall, parallel to the foot of the elderly man's bed. A black woman, young and attractive, perhaps his wife, sits in a chair near him. She rises and adjusts his pillow. She talks softly and smooths his top sheet. We must have disturbed him with our conversation. We hush.

The suffocating odor of Lysol drifts in from the hallway where the night cleaning crew quickly swish their mops across the grey-flecked vinyl floors. I prefer Pine-Sol but no one asks me. I chuckle to myself, thankful that my sense of humor is still intact. Somehow I force myself into a sleep state and escape the acrid odors.

When the nauseating smell of sizzling bacon awakens me, stomach acid rushes up my esophagus burning my throat and nostrils. Heaving up last night's supper I manage to hang my head over the railing and vomit onto the clean mopped floor. I fumble for my call button. Every cell in my body screams with convulsions. Somewhere on the night stand is the kidney-shaped plastic dish for just such emergencies. Sorry. Maybe next time. Thus begins my first day after Christmas.

A nurse hurries to my bedside and dabs a wet wash cloth over my face. A woman rolls her mop bucket through the door and cleans up the mess on the floor. I can't understand what the women are saying, but the cleaning woman opens the blinds. I welcome the daylight as my stomach settles down.

"Have you seen Tanya this morning? Is she able to eat? Can she keep it down?" I hope so. The nurse promises to check on my daughter.

"Tell her I love her. Always tell her I love her." She smiles and nods. When she returns she says that Tanya asked the same questions about me. That's a good sign. We'll survive together. *Hang in there, honey.*

"Mrs. Proctor, your son is here," the nurse tells me as she pushes a stretcher alongside my bed. "We're taking you to x-ray but he can go with you."

I remember that Richard said something about Ricky, Mike, and Mike's wife Janice flying in from Texas this morning. Before they were married Janice spent our family vacation with us at Robbers' Cave State Park near Wilburton, Oklahoma. A couple of years later she and Mike were married at Hutto, Texas, while we were living in Germany. Richard's parents stood in for us as parents–rather grandparents–of the groom.

Ricky steps forward and mutters, "Hi, Mom." Gritting his teeth to steady his nerves, as is his habit, he sucks in a deep breath and lets it out all at once. "Mike and Janice are with Tanya. Dad's talking to Tanya's doctor."

I recognize the emotion-laden tone of his Texas drawl. The nurse shakes my bed when she lowers the bed rail. I moan. Ricky grimaces. "What do you need me to do for you, Mom?" He asks me, but looks to the nurse for an answer.

"Could you help me lift your mother onto this cart?" Ricky quickly responds. "Take hold of the draw sheet at her feet like this." Ricky grips the sheet on both sides of my feet, and, in one coordinated movement, the two of them swing me onto the stretcher. The motion was less painful than I had anticipated. I'm glad to be out of my bed for a while.

Lying on my back as we leave the room, I try to notice where we're going. People and walls flash by too quickly like mirrored reflections in a fun house tunnel. I laugh to keep from giving in to motion sickness. Without my trifocals I see only blurred images. It's good to have Ricky with me.

We don't have to wait long in radiology. The technician tries to position me for the x-ray angles the doctor ordered. My hip feels like a monster's claw is ripping into the flesh. "Oh, wait," I yell. "I can't turn this way." Yet somehow I manage the torturous angles for a couple more x-rays. I close my eyes and try to stand the pain. Ricky can tolerate my groans no longer. I hear his western boots walking away. In an agitated voice he demands, "My mother has got to have something for her pain. Whatever you're giving her isn't working."

A nurse appears with a hypodermic needle. "Son, you just let me know anything your mother needs," she says as she draws up the liquid into the syringe. I hope the medication will take effect quickly. Thank goodness Ricky spoke up for me. By the time they return me to my room and lift me into my bed the medication is doing its job. Pain is fatiguing and I'm exhausted.

Mike and Janice tiptoe in quietly. "Tanya said for you to come on down," Mike whispers to Ricky. "Her door is open."

Ricky's eyes brighten at the mention of his sister's name. "I love you, Mom. See you later."

"I love you, too, Ricky. Thanks for helping to lift me this morning." I hear the spring in his step as he heads for the door.

Mike's eyes are red and swollen. He tries to smile. Janice looks like she could use some sleep, too. I regret the horrible nights they have spent since they were notified about our tragedy. Janice holds a foil wrapped flower pot with a purple bow.

"Mike said you like African violets. We thought this one was the prettiest," she says as she sets the plant on my bedside table. It's the first of many plants and flowers I will receive. I ask a lot of questions about their flight, about Janice's family, about where they were when Richard phoned. Mike says very little. Perhaps his visit with Tanya has drained him emotionally. Mike was always our most sensitive child. As the oldest son he felt responsible for his brothers' and sisters' whether or not they appreciated his concern.

After Mike and Janice leave I can't shake the haunting image of Mike's sad eyes. No one will ever take Terry Glen's place in Mike's life and I know that. What I didn't know was that Terry Glen's body had been cremated before Mike arrived.

Richard, Tanya, and I had talked with Reverend Gisselbeck about cremation because we didn't know where we should have the boys and babies interred. Being an army family we had no permanent home. The funeral director informed us that the funeral home would keep the ashes for as long as we needed to leave them in their possession. That seemed like a reasonable solution at the time.

Unfortunately Mike didn't get to say his good-byes to Terry Glen or to his youngest brother Roger. Young Roger had grown into a good looking adolescent during the nearly four years since Mike last saw him at Tanya's and Bob's wedding. Communication had become garbled in our tragedy. Time stopped. Decisions were made. Unfortunately bodies were cremated without regard to the emotional needs of family members arriving from out of state. It wasn't anyone's fault. We simply had not traveled down this road before and now we were clumsily finding our way. Mike and Ricky had desperately needed to see their brothers one last time. *Lord, help us.*

Soon Richard came in and took his tired family home. Somehow he must make sleeping arrangements for them in the home where they had never lived but where their brothers lived a very short time. I longed to go home with them.

"Were those your sons?" The mother of a teenage boy whose bed stands parallel to the foot of my bed had watched my family come and go. She tells me that her seventeen-year-old son had suffered head injuries in a motorcycle accident. His mind is confused, but she is able to understand him and soothe his anxiety. I notice his bruised face but there are no bandages or casts. Like the elderly man who shares our ward, the boy is here for close medical observation. At least the woman's son is alive. I wish that Terry Glen and Roger were alive, too, and sharing my room. All of us could go home together.

In the night I hear the boy mumbling. I see him shaking his head as though the words won't come out right. He throws the sheet to the side and rummages under his pillow. Maybe he's searching for the call button penned to his bed. I can help. I ring for the nurse. She comes immediately.

"I'll be with you in a moment, Mrs. Proctor, but first I must see what he needs." I tell her I only rang for him and not for myself. I'm okay. It gratifies me to know that, in my limited condition, I can still help someone else–another mother's son.

The next day Richard comes alone to see me. We needed time together. The large crowd at home was now looking after Sheilia. Richard wouldn't have to drive that thirty-mile trip to Carroll County hospital anymore. But something else was on his mind. I knew that look.

"Sheilia saw Terry Glen and Roger after the accident," he says, "but she thought the covered bodies on the ground were from the other vehicle. At the hospital, when the ambulance didn't bring them in, she slowly realized those bodies were Terry Glen and Roger. Then she told Ruth Ross that she had glimpsed heaven.

"What did she mean?" I wondered aloud. A chill rolled through my body.

"Sheilia said she was caught up in space and felt extremely happy. She saw Roger and Terry Glen. People dressed in biblical robes were coming toward them. Roger looked at her and she sensed his thoughts. 'Sister, I know something you don't.' "

"She said that somehow she knew that these people had come to take Terry Glen and Roger to the Lord. She wanted to go with them but she must return to the living."

No one in our family had ever experienced a near death encounter with persons who were already dead. "When she feels well enough to ride in the car, bring her to me," I said. I must hear her tell me in her own words what she saw and heard.

Roger and Sheilia were especially close to each other after our tour in Israel last year. As for Terry Glen he often meditated alone. It wasn't the children's spirituality that bothered me. Yet I couldn't explain this happening.

A few days later my pale, thin daughter sat by my bed and told me of her extraordinary experience. "Mom, I felt so happy. I felt like, 'Wow! I made it!' I thought of all the things I had wanted to do in this life, but nothing compared with the joy I felt." Her face was radiant.

"When Roger looked at me and I knew I had to come back, I tried to dig in my heels. Some force was pulling me backwards. I didn't want to leave them. Then I heard a man's voice. He told me to hand him the baby." The baby was Paula lying in a heap on her lap in our vehicle.

Her shoulders slumped as Sheilia looked down at the heavy casts on her arms. I was grateful that Ruth Ross had been the first person to whom Sheilia confided her story. She shared it with no one else outside the family.

Left to right: Roger, Richard, Martha, and Sheilia who is carrying a bottle filled with water from the Jordan River after her baptism, April, 1981.

In the meantime, when Tanya was able to talk without tubes or oxygen she related a similar experience to Richard. "Tanya said she saw Becky, then Paula, and Ruth Ann floating toward her with other people. As they floated past her she saw them moving toward a glow." Richard had to swallow before he could say more.

"Tanya said the children were not afraid. They seemed to feel safe with the other people or presences. She tried to go with them but something held her back, like a hand on her shoulder."

Like an angel or a rescuer or a doctor or nurse? Between our daughters' experiences everyone who died was encountered spiritually before we were rescued. God comforted Tanya about her children and Sheilia about her brothers in a way that I could not. I was the driver of our vehicle yet I could not save them. I tried but failed. My sons and granddaughters died trusting their lives to me.

The next week blurred into continuous pain and hospital routines made bearable by the welcome visits from my family and ministers. Richard said that reporters knocked on our neighbors' doors on Christmas day. Why did they have to ruin Christmas for our friends like that? Couldn't they have waited till the next day?

My left ear continued to drain. I couldn't hear. The doctor said my right cheek bone was fractured leaving the right eye slightly displaced downward. Surgery could restore it, but I risked blindness. With limited hearing, strained eyesight, and a persistent headache, I withdrew into my own thoughts, trying to grasp what had happened and where we were headed.

We decided to postpone the funeral until Tanya and I were dismissed from the hospital. She and I felt we must be present at the memorial service. With the help of Reverend Gisselbeck and our doctors we set the date for January 10. Tanya and I applied ourselves to our painful physical therapy regimens with grit and determination. Just getting out of bed and into a wheelchair was a major operation. I struggled with crutches and stairs. Tanya eventually managed a walker dragging her leg encased in a cast.

I was told that at home Linda had pinned phone messages on the kitchen bulletin board. She and Janice handled the cooking, laundry, and cleaning. Linda roasted the turkey I had planned to serve on Christmas day. Terry mopped and waxed the kitchen floor. I'm sure crumbs from the children's last meal were scattered under the table. I didn't take time to sweep them up before we left for Westminster.

Competing demands limited Richard's time with Tanya and me. Lawyers, police, and insurance claims adjustors required him to answer endless questions, and fill out countless forms. Reporters phoned the house, the hospital, and church daily. The world rushed in and we were engulfed.

Holiday traffic jammed the roads to Baltimore frustrating Richard on his daily trips to the hospital to be with Tanya and me. A blinding rainstorm stalled traffic one morning and he later told me that he felt the dam cracking inside him which held back a rising tide of emotions. He pulled off the road, turned off the key, and gave way to the flood of tears which sapped his strength.

"All heaven seemed to be crying with me," he said. "I was immobilized with crying for some time."

In the midst of everything the water pump at the house malfunctioned. *Roger will help his dad install a new one. Oh, my gosh! Roger's dead.* I couldn't get used to the thought. We had bought the house last summer when Roger voted for it out of the several houses we were shown by the realtor. A 3,000-acre state park bordered on our back fence and a small red brick barn housed the riding lawnmower Roger operated to mow the acre-and-a-half lot. He was a great handyman, helping his dad to paint and paper the dining room and learning to do minor repair jobs.

We'll miss you, Roger. You were our bonus baby in so many wonderful ways.

Reverend Ruth Ross brought me a tape of her sermon today titled, "The Risk of Birth." "I didn't know how my sermon would affect Richard," she said, looking at me with those compassionate grey eyes and gentle smile. I didn't expect to see him and his sister in the congregation this morning."

"I needed to hear it," Richard said, "and I want you to hear her sermon, too." Richard thought Ruth Ross was the best woman preacher he had ever heard. Her sermons always went one step deeper than the listener expected. To him she served as an alter ego. Sheilia also marveled that Reverend Ross understood so well the issues that concerned teens. I suspect her wisdom came from her experience in rearing her own five teenagers.

The next day Ruth suffered severe internal pains on her way home from the church. She drove to the emergency room and a few hours later she underwent abdominal surgery. Reverend Gisselbeck was quickly losing his staff and expanding his hospital visits.

During the week church members drove thirty miles from Westminster in ice and snow to deliver food to our Clarksburg home. Neighbors we barely knew provided more. Janice started filling the freezer in the basement and kindly asked them to bring no more food. Richard even brought a slice of German chocolate cake to me. Chocolate cake, of any kind, is my favorite.

With dessert he also brought my Christmas presents, one gift each day. As I unwrapped Roger's box I recalled how he learned about Hanukkah from his kindergarten friend John-John. That year Richard admonished our children that if they didn't hold down the decibel level and frenetic activity they wouldn't get any Christmas gifts. Five-year-old Roger exclaimed, "You mean we're going to have Hanukkah?" John-John had told him that Jewish children receive one gift each day during Hanukkah. That sounded good to Roger. Now I'm the person opening one gift each day but Hanukkah and Christmas are both past.

Ironically, the gift Roger had purchased for me was a pair of white marble paperweights with slogans stamped in black on top. "Why me, Lord?" and "Do it tomorrow. You've made enough mistakes today." The humor was lost in the prophetic messages.

Linda brought her own gift the next day. Her fever was gone and she was due to fly home tomorrow. "I thought you might like something soft and fuzzy to cuddle," she said as she handed me "Bear Hug", a honey-colored teddy bear. "I gave Tanya a fuzzy stuffed Bugs Bunny," she laughed.

Linda is the prime contributor to my teddy bear collection. Ever since I gave her my blue and white panda Bobinkus when I married her brother twenty-six years ago she has tried to replace Bobinkus for me. I suspected that Linda, a ten-year-old at that time, thought the panda was a fair exchange for her brother. Today she believes that everyone should have a teddy bear.

I was grateful for the many people who made it possible for our out-of-state family members to be with us. No one has spare cash at Christmas. Yet like the loaves and fishes offered by the young boy to Jesus to feed the multitudes who gathered for his Sermon on the Mount, the means were multiplied.

Kerry Freeman, a fellow Boy Scout with Richard and Terry, brought cash to Linda and Terry in Tulsa for airline tickets. Janice's family enabled Mike and Janice to buy tickets to come at once. God was watching over us in His mysterious ways.

Linda returned to her family in Denver and Terry returned to his home in Houston. Mike and Janice, Ricky and Bob continued to await Tanya's and my release from the hospital. The days dragged on, like a caterpillar earth-mover, reshaping the landscape of our lives.

Public Reaction

"Lest they drink and forget the law; and
pervert the judgment of any of the afflicted."
- Proverbs 31:5 KJV

Wrapped in a strange cocoon of timelessness, stillness, and uncertainty, I lay suspended somewhere between waking and dreaming, the region where poets and storytellers collect troubling images and create new stories. This is a story I do not want to write.

Richard left some newspaper articles with me about the accident. "Family Trip to Christmas Eve Service Ends in Tragedy, *Washington Post*. "Holiday Tragedy Called Worst Accident in County History," *Carroll County Times*. "5 Are Killed En Route to Christmas Play," *The Baltimore Sun*.

Photos hastily supplied by Richard are featured of Terry Glen, Roger, and Sheilia. A close-up of Terry Glen in the studio Christmas portrait taken five years ago strikes a bittersweet note. *Terry Glen I feared you could be killed in Korea. I never dreamed you would die riding beside me on a road close to home.* Pictures of Terry Glen in Korea are still stored in the boxes we have yet to unpack since we returned from Germany.

Sheilia's senior picture will be published in the Damascus High School annual next spring. Roger's photo with his soccer team calls to mind the art project in which he designed a shield depicting his interests in sports. In one corner he wrote his epitaph telling how he wished to be remembered. "He was a good athlete. Too bad the poor boy died."

Yes, Roger, your teammates, especially Sean Parker and Deke Burt, will always remember you as a star athlete. Richard said Sean's mother phoned to schedule a visit with Roger during the holidays. She was horrified to learn of our tragedy. They had been gone for Christmas and had not heard the news.

Ironically, the most complete article was written by the reporters whom Richard allowed into our home Christmas night. "I couldn't cry," Richard was quoted as saying. "I was raised in a family where boys didn't cry. But when I studied medicine, I learned that wasn't right. I cry in private. I cried with my brother and sister today." Richard had told me of their crying together at Mount Airy when they identified the bodies. The news men had listened after all. Now I realized that it had helped Richard to be able to talk about his sons. *Lord, forgive me for being quick to judge.*

When I see the quotes from my neighbors, however, I feel guilty for ruining their Christmas. I want everything to be like it was before we left home for church on Christmas Eve. If only I had left an hour later. If only I hadn't been so obsessively punctual. I wanted to be sure that no detail had been overlooked for the evening's performance.

I wanted Tanya to be comfortably seated on the bale of alfalfa hay so Ruth Ann would be settled before the congregation came along to pause at the makeshift stable. I wanted to take Terry Glen on a tour of all the classrooms prepared for the Journey to Bethlehem pageant. If only . . . .

"Christmas did not come for the Proctor family," wrote an editor. What? Can he be right? Is Christmas no deeper than the tinsel trashed the day after? True, the Bible speaks of tragedy that first Christmas when King Herod ordered every male infant slaughtered. For those mothers Christmas was not wrapped in swaddling clothes but in shrouds. For Tanya and me, also.

Yet somewhere in the star-crossed side of Christmas lies the balm for my grieving soul. I am persuaded that Christmas has been interrupted but not cancelled for my family. In that moment my detoured Journey to Bethlehem is transformed from a pageant into a spiritual odyssey, a search for the true meaning of this Christmas for my grieving family. Like Simeon waiting in the temple to see the infant Savior, or the wise men from the East following the star, I begin my quest.

Opening the blue leather bound King James Bible in large print which Richard bought for me, I turn to the family register. Marriages, Births, Deaths. I simply cannot write my sons and granddaughters' names in the death registry. It's too soon. I still feel their presence, hear their voices, see the boys stacking their gifts under the tree while Becky and Paula rearrange the olive wood nativity figures in the bay window. The spotless death register page remains blank.

I read another article. The public outrage is immense. A high school principal pleads for community action. His column, "We Can Stop the Maiming," sounds like a rallying cry– STOP THE MAIMING. He argues that committed citizens can do it, as does MADD, Mothers Against Drunk Driving. Oddly, I don't feel the rage yet, just homesickness, pain, and fatigue.

Richard says there are no bad people, only good people who do bad things. So, what's the answer? More studies? Tougher laws? Re-education? The *News American* article, "Defeating the Drunk Driver, an Uphill Fight," identifies obstacles to effective solutions. The *Carroll County Times* states that, "Police Say Judge, States Too Soft on Drunken Drivers."

I cringe at the formidable task ahead and fear that we will be overwhelmed by well-intended crusaders. Our private grief work stands to be sidetracked. I must regain control of my life. I must reach my arms around my family and restore our smaller family circle. We are not fragmented individuals but still a whole family.

As New Year's Eve approaches, Sam Donaldson's staff contacts Richard. Would he be willing to be interviewed on New Year's Eve in Washington, D.C.? The presentation could save lives. Reluctantly, Richard agrees. He scans statistical reports on alcohol-related accidents at the national and local levels. MADD is active in nine states including Maryland. If Richard, a bereaved father and grandfather, shares his tragedy, surely holiday drinkers will think twice before getting behind the steering wheel. Maybe someone will be spared dying under the wheels of a drunk driver.

The nursing staff arrange for Tanya and me to watch the live interview together on a TV set mounted on Tanya's wall. As the nurse wheels me down the hallway, I feel anxious. My hands are clammy. I haven't seen my daughter since she and I were removed from the crash site. The distance from my room to hers is shorter than I expected. If I had been propelling my wheelchair myself, I'm certain I would have screeched the brakes when I saw her through the open door to her room. Propped up high in her bed, her right leg is in traction, both arms hidden in casts she looks like a patched up rag doll with a smiling face.

A sense of dejá vu sweeps me back to a time when Tanya was nine months old and I stayed at the hospital bedside of my Granny, the sixty-five-year old victim of a drunk driver. Granny lingered for months in excruciating pain. Her doctor presented her case to a young intern and remarked, "We didn't expect her to live."

Granny pulled herself up on her elbows and admonished her faithful physician. "Doctor, I had no intentions of dying" . . . as though the decision was entirely her own to make. To everyone's surprise, Granny lived nineteen more years, sewing outfits for her great-grandchildren. The last item she stitched was a flannel infant nightgown for Tanya's baby Becky.

I choke as tears wash my face. "Tanya, I'm so sorry. . . ."

"Mom, you did all you could do," she quickly replies. "It wasn't your fault." That settles it for now. We'll talk later when we're safe at home again. For now it is enough that we are together and receiving good medical care.

We chat about how good everyone has been to us. Knowing that our extended family and friends are gathered around their TV sets tonight to hear what Richard has to say, I feel we are gathered in a large invisible company of supportive viewers.

Nurses and aides tend to our needs and wait with us. TV commercials blare wildly as the old year1981 comes to a close. Sam Donaldson looks at the camera and speaks. A crumpled chunk of metal that had been our new VW Rabbit station wagon appears on the screen. In my shock I don't hear Sam anymore.

"How did we survive?" Tanya cries out. The mangled heap looks like a beer can crushed by a road grader–just like Granny's old Buick appeared in the photo which Uncle Leroy snapped of her wreckage. Like Granny, I, too, lay unconscious in the smoldering wreckage while men operated chainsaws to get each of us out. How, indeed, did any one of us survive?

If our family had driven to Westminster in two automobiles, perhaps more of us would have lived. Or would both vehicles have been wrecked by the sudden appearance of the 1969 Plymouth in our lane? As for child restraint laws, it would be 1983 before accidents, such as ours, gave sufficient impetus to the increasing demand for such legislation. Who would have thought that a baby would not be safe in her mother's arms? Obviously we didn't. Yet Tanya's babies and brothers became a statistic on Christmas Eve. Terry Glen and I had buckled up in the front seat when we left home, but the law did not require backseat passengers to do so.

More rebuttals flash through my mind as I watch the interview in progress. Richard looks grim and lonely. The fact is he *was* alone, he told me later. He was seated in a studio room, facing a camera, watching a TV monitor. Sam Donaldson was filming in New York. There was no face-to-face encounter. When Richard does not demand blood–justice, whatever that might have been–the host immediately interrupts him. The camera pans to a member of MADD who continues the interview and Richard is not heard from again. Now I'm the one who is angry.

Richard had pleaded for personal responsibility. If you drink, don't drive. Obviously that was *not* the script the TV host expected to hear. Why did he bother to interview Richard, if he had his own agenda? The photo of the crushed vehicle and the presence of a grieving man would draw viewers. But a call for moral commitment would turn them off. Since when did driving under the influence of alcohol become the right of a licensed driver? I was learning first hand that victims have no rights.

Before Richard agreed to be filmed, we discussed our views. He found that more people were killed by drunk drivers in the United States in 1981 than were killed in eight years of the Viet Nam War. We didn't want to see the young offender treated as a scape goat for society's problem with alcohol. More than likely, he was only one of hundreds driving drunk in Maryland that night.

My mind raced on. Laws are not enough. Laws are not enforced. Attitudes must change. Personal responsibility must be taught. It's easier to blame society, blame the industry, blame TV. Does the person who cherishes his freedom really want the courts to decide for him what should be his personal responsibility?

The aide turns off the TV. Discussion is brief. Tanya and I are told we must sleep now. As the nurse wheels me back to my room I contemplate the significance of what I have heard and seen tonight. Richard and I have been thrown into a national issue we did not choose. Having landed there, we must fight not to be used as pawns. Perhaps we should state our views in a letter to the editor or submit an essay to the guest columnist. At least editors seem more inclined to print alternative viewpoints.

However, it is past midnight. The New Year has begun. I resolve to speak for the dead, live for the living, and fully recover. My conscience warns, "Don't hate." My instinct roars, "I'm mad as hell."

Terry Glen (*left*) and Ricky (*right*) with Granny
(Vera Faye Huchel) outside her cabin at Robber's
Cave State Park, Wilburton, Oklahoma, July, 1978.
Ricky is wearing a shirt and vest Granny made for him.

$\diamondsuit$ 6

Miracles Still Happen

"And he [Jesus] said, 'The things which are impossible
with men, are possible with God."
                                    - Luke 18:27 KJV

Sunday, January 3, 1982. "Richard laid hands on my head
and prayed for my healing." If I were journaling that's what I
would write. Three days have passed since Richard's TV interview
on New Year's Eve and my head hasn't stopped throbbing, nor my
ear draining.

The surgeon intends to surgically repair my fractured right
eye socket tomorrow. I've signed the consent forms but the risk of
blindness concerns me. My right eye was my good eye until the
accident. My left eye provides only 10% vision. I've worn glasses
since I was thirteen and trifocals the past several years.

I was feeling blue about all this when Richard arrived late
this afternoon. I expected to see my sister Joan Rodgers with him
but he was alone. Joan was flying standby from Tulsa on an
American Airlines pass since her husband Olan is an employee of
the airlines.

"Joan's still trying to get out of the Dallas-Fort Worth
airport where she had to change planes," Richard explains. "She's
anxious to see you before you undergo surgery.".

"Richard, I feel uneasy about the surgery. I know it's inevitable, but I'm not ready for it. What about Walter Reed? Do you think they would do it?"

An army wife, loyal to the end, I thought I might feel more comfortable among army medical personnel at Walter Reed Army Medical Center. However, I had nothing but praise for the life-saving treatment Tanya and I had received at the University of Maryland trauma center. Since it was a holiday week-end Richard would not be able to check with Walter Reed until tomorrow.

"Also, I want you to lay hands on me and pray for my healing." If God could transport our daughters to heavenly visions in near death experiences, surely the Almighty would hear our prayers for my recovery.

We prayed for a safe flight for Joan before we prayed for our own needs. Then I closed my eyes and prayed silently while Richard examined my face. The tips of his fingers moved gently over the swollen bumps on my left eye socket as he prayed aloud. The firm pressure of his warm hands was like a potter's steady touch, shaping the clay on the whirling wheel. I felt no pain.

Richard had scarcely said, "Amen," when the phone rang. Mike was calling from home to say that Joan was waiting for Richard at Dulles Airport. Seems Joan had poured out her story to another passenger who helped her to get rerouted through Raleigh, North Carolina. Do miracles really happen that quickly? I hoped this was a good sign. Richard kissed me good night and left for the airport. I knew I would sleep well. As for tomorrow I trusted that Walter Reed would have a room for me and that the outcome of my surgery would be completely in the hands of God. I slept soundly without medication.

Monday morning, January 4, 1982. I really should start journaling. So much has happened. The doctor popped in and gave me the good news that Walter Reed is dispatching an army ambulance for me. I called home and told Richard and Joan to meet

48

me at Walter Reed. Joan nearly cried when I talked to her but she's glad I'm being transferred. They won't have to drive so far.

"Mrs. Proctor, it looks like everything is in order," the cheery nurse says as she bags my few belongings and looks over some papers. "Would you like to stop by Tanya's room while we're waiting for the ambulance?"

She helps me into my wheelchair. I'm still slow, but I'm getting better at managing my transfer from bed to chair. How does Tanya do it, weighted down with three casts? Yesterday an aide wheeled her into my room for a short visit. I was amazed. Tanya was cheery, putting up a good front. I knew the act. She's her mother's daughter. We both laughed to keep from crying.

I feel sad at leaving her behind. It's been comforting to know she was just down the hall. When I rolled into her room I was glad to see the many flowers she had received.

"Guess you won't need any of my potted plants," I said. Tanya loves to garden. At home she often picnicked with Becky and Paula on a blanket at the edge of our garden, giving the children small butter tubs for collecting tiny wild flowers and clover.

"I'll be praying for you, Mom," she promises.

"And I'll be praying for you, honey. We'll both be home soon," I hope. We wave good-by and the nurse wheels me out the door. This time as we go down the corridor I notice the brightly painted walls, shiny floor tiles, and rush of people hurrying in and out of rooms. I need a map to locate where I am and where I've been. However I won't need it anymore.

Everyone has been kind, but I'm glad to get outside and breathe fresh air. Two army medical specialists are waiting to help me onto a stretcher. They lift me into the ambulance and firmly secure the safety belts. As the driver pulls out onto the street my pain returns. Every pot hole and wicked crack in the pavement reverberates through my fractured bones. I fear the meager improvement I have made will be undone.

"Ooh, isn't there an easier way to go?" I plead. The driver watches me in the rear view mirror as I grip the stretcher and clench my jaw.

"Didn't they give you a painkiller before we left? There's not much I can do about these streets," he says apologetically. "I'm trying to avoid the worst holes."

"I don't know what they gave me. I just know that I'm bouncing all over the place back here," I moan.

The attendant does his best to steady the stretcher even though it is strapped securely. I want Richard to come get me. I just know that he would be able to transport me more comfortably in our VW camper. At that thought I laugh to myself, even as I am jolted and hurting. Richard would have to drive over the same roads and I probably wouldn't feel one bit better.

The ambulance driver pulls off the road. The attendant tries to adjust the stretcher again. I feel ashamed at making such a fuss. "I'll be okay," I promise. "I've driven this road myself and I know how bad it is. You just keep trying to miss those holes and I'll keep hanging on. We'll make it."

The driver swings back into traffic and the distance seems shorter, if no less excruciating, as we talk about the weather instead of the bumpy road. Soon he announces that we are entering the gate at Walter Reed. I look up through the window at the bare branches of the old trees and hope that I will be able to see them in the spring when they shade the blooming azaleas that cover the hospital grounds.

A few minutes later I wave good-by to my escorts as a nurse whisks me away in a wheelchair to meet the surgeon. He takes me directly to x-ray and orders a head shot. Then the nurse wheels me to my private room where a matronly black aide is adjusting the blinds.

"Mrs. Williams will help you get settled. The doctor will be in just as soon as he studies your x-rays."

After being confined to my tiny screened cubicle in intensive care at the shock trauma unit, I find this room to be quite large. Mrs. Williams lowers the bed so I won't have to step up. When I become agitated because I can't lie in any position without pressure on my hip, she knows exactly what I need. She locates a foam rubber "egg crate" and remakes my bed while I sit in the wheelchair. In a few minutes I'm grateful for the amazing difference such a simple pad makes. Mine got left behind in Baltimore.

My head is throbbing. My hip feels like the jagged corner of a cardboard box is inside piercing through the muscle. Mrs. Williams helps me find a comfortable position. No sooner has she propped up my pillows and rolled up the head of my bed than the surgeon enters my room smiling and shaking his head.

"From the looks of your x-rays you might not need surgery after all. I notified the chief of plastic surgery and he wants to examine you himself."

Can this be true? I'm afraid to hope. The chief comes in wearing his white coat and holding my chart. After introducing himself he tilts my face and studies it carefully.

"How are you going to improve on that?" he says to the other physician. "If she were my own wife, I wouldn't operate."

The chief explains that the swelling has gone down. The cartilage has been perfectly repositioned. The x-rays confirm it. Of course I tell him at once about Richard's laying hands on my face and praying. Regardless of what the physicians expected, they acknowledge that something good has happened. Now they want to know about my other injuries. Unfortunately my hospital records did not accompany me from Baltimore.

"I forgot about my other injuries," I laugh. Then I tell them about my dislocated hip and fractured pelvis, the persistent headaches, blood draining from my left ear, and my loss of hearing in that ear.

"Good grief. How did you forget all of that?"

"I was so worried about the possibility of blindness that nothing else mattered." I'm ecstatic. My stomach growls and I realize I'm actually hungry. Since no surgery will be scheduled I can eat lunch. When my tray is delivered I devour every crumb and find that my sense of taste has returned also.

After lunch an attendant brings a wheelchair to my room and rolls me back to the x-ray lab again. "Since your records still haven't arrived from the other hospital," he says, "the doctors ordered x-rays of your other injuries." At this point I don't care how many times I must move from the bed to the wheelchair, as long as I can see. Now I don't have to fear going blind.

When we enter the crowded waiting room I feel uneasy to learn that I have been squeezed into the schedule ahead of all these other people. My euphoria wears off when my hip goes into spasm, my escort leaves, and the x-ray technician growls, "Lady, just step up on that footstool and sit down on the table."

I manage to pull myself up out of the wheelchair only to look down at the footstool which might as well be a mountain. It looks so high for a single step. Pain immobilizes my hip and my feet stay riveted to the floor.

"Lady, just tell me what to do and I'll help you," he snaps.

"I don't know what to do." I feel so helpless. "I've never been hurt like this before." I want to cry but I don't. I want to step up easily and sit down like I always did before . . . before I couldn't. I wish Ricky was here to help me. The technician walks over beside me and waits for me to think this through. Somehow, with his patience, I manage to climb the mountain and sit down on the cold, hard surface. With a minimum of groaning I survive the positions for the x-rays. The technician carefully helps me down the mountain and into my wheelchair. Back in my room I give myself credit for having climbed my first step since the accident.

The next morning I begin physical therapy. Crying my way through the first session I remember my grandmother's screams in physical therapy twenty years ago. She would tell the specialist,

"Don't pay any attention to my yells. I won't beat you when I can walk again." What courage she had. But as for me I can't stop sobbing.

"Do you want to go back to your room?" the woman asks.

"No, I can cry as well here as in my bed. I must keep trying. Please, ignore my tears."

So far I can't even pull myself up to a standing position with the crutches, much less take a step. To make matters worse, I'm the only cry baby in the group. A man walks quickly on artificial legs down a short aisle with a railing on each side. At the end of the aisle, a full length mirror allows him to see how well his new legs are working. On a mat, a woman without arms or legs tosses her torso around to strengthen her muscles so she can be fitted with artificial limbs. At least my pain lets me know that I still *have* arms and legs and even a hip that will eventually heal. I WILL walk again.

The physical therapist helps me create a personal task list. I make a note to ask Richard to count the steps at home which I will need to walk from the car to the front porch, up the stairs onto the porch, and the paces across the porch to the front door. Each distance is a separate task. Now I can measure my progress each day as I learn to walk with crutches. It sounds so simple. It hurts so much. It seems so far.

While my attention is focused on the enormity of the job before me, Reverend Gisselbeck comes in for a cheerful visit. "You actually wrote out instructions for getting into and out of the car?" he asks. "I never thought about how I do that. It's just automatic."

"That's because you've never been in this condition where every muscle must be persuaded to function in spite of the pain." I was proud of my step-by-step instructions. "Do you know how Tanya is getting along with her exercises?"

"The staff say that Tanya is astounding everyone," he reports. "She even agreed to let them videotape her sessions for teaching purposes."

Secretly, I suspect that Tanya is running a race with me to see who will get home first. *Bless her heart. Okay. I'll play the game.*

In the meantime a trapeze is attached to the head of my bed and provides leverage for me to raise myself to a sitting position. One morning just as the nurse is leaving I reach for the trapeze and hear a loud crack. The nurse whirls around.

"What happened?"

Still hanging on to the trapeze I let go and then I feel it. "It's my shoulder but it doesn't hurt as bad as it sounded." Nevertheless back to x-ray I go. Allowed to wait my turn for a change I sit there reasoning that a hairline fracture probably existed undiscovered until I stressed it with my grip on the trapeze.

"You're right," the doctor says. "You snapped your right scapula. It should heal without treatment if you don't try anymore acrobatics."

Next stop is the ophthalmologist's office. He finds no glass fragments in my eyes even though there are cuts on my forehead. I can thank the makers of safety glass windshields for that. I don't understand though how my glasses were broken and my nose wasn't.

Back in my room a familiar face from Germany rolls in seated in her wheelchair. June Eitel, who lived a few houses up the street from us at Kelley Barracks is a terminally ill cancer patient at Walter Reed. June tells me she begged her doctor to let her pay a visit to me as soon as her medication gave her some respite from her pain. June and her husband, Colonel Eitel, were on leave in the states when we moved into their housing area three years ago. Both of June's parents died and one of her husband's parents died before they returned to Kelley Barracks at the end of the summer. When I met June for the first time, under those circumstances, all I could say was, "I'm so sorry." Trying to find some mutual ground for friendship I had added, "My middle name is June, also."

Now she is here consoling me when I should be comforting her. "Time does heal," June says. "I didn't think it could at the time I lost my parents. But trust me, Martha June. Time will lessen your grief." She seems to be at peace, smiling as she talks. When she left I knew sadly that I would never see her again. But I would treasure her memory always.

One morning a nurse noticed a partial paralysis of the left side of my face. She left the room and returned with the doctor. He looked concerned but said the distortion most likely would be temporary. Maybe only a few days. He told the nurse to check it each day. I hadn't seen myself in a mirror since the accident so I was unaware of the paralysis. I ran my fingertips over my cheek and asked for a mirror. Sure enough the smile in my heart did not appear on my face. Just a twisted grimace. I hoped the doctor was right that this condition would be temporary.

I couldn't sleep that night. I declined sleeping pills, preferring meditation. But it wasn't working. Fear intruded. Tears washed my cheeks, but my paralyzed cheek felt nothing. I needed someone to talk to.

Please, Lord, send me a prayer partner.

A Filipino nurse who shared her faith with me earlier this week was on duty. She appeared in my doorway. "Are you okay?" she asked. "I was writing at the nurses' station when something prompted me to come to you."

"I'm having a pity party," I sniffle. "I look so horrendous. People will stay away from me."

"If you mean that people will pity you, that's right. You must prepare yourself for that." *I want sympathy and she gives me advice instead.*

"You must understand where they're coming from. They don't want to hurt you, but they won't be able to hide their shock.

It's up to you to put them at ease." *So she's telling me that I'm the one in control?*

"You know your paralysis will heal. They don't know that. You must reassure them and drop it. Talk about them instead."

She sounds like a mom talking to her adolescent daughter but she's right. I can change my situation by changing my attitude. Just knowing that makes me feel better. This faith business is demanding more of me than I had bargained for.

Ten days after the accident blood still oozes from my left ear and I still can't hear in that ear. My tension headaches continue. So seldom do I have headaches that Richard can banish them with a kiss on my temple. But his kisses aren't working their usual magic. We better tell the physician.

A CAT scan reveals a skull fracture in the lower left mastoid area. There is nothing that can be done except to wait and let nature take its course. The memorial service is scheduled for Sunday and I'm determined to be there. Tanya has already been discharged. I feel ashamed that she won our race. Her injuries were much worse than mine.

My other sister Ruth Lance is flying in today for the memorial service. Joan's husband Olan will be here overnight. I bolster my spirits by checking my progress list. I can walk with crutches now. I can manage up the stairs and down the stairs. When the physician saw me in the stairwell yesterday morning under the supervision of the physical therapist he looked surprised. I told him, "I'm getting out here." But now it seems the unsuspected skull fracture could delay my release.

Richard manages to persuade the physician to give me a hospital pass for the week-end on the promise that he will bring me back Monday for observation. With the assurance that I will be going home tomorrow I look forward to the family's visiting me tonight.

Around seven o'clock I hear their voices outside my door. Richard and Mike walk in smiling, followed by Ruth, Joan, and

Olan. Janice stayed home with Tanya and Sheilia. Olan nods to me and diverts his eyes to the floor. I realize that my crooked face distresses him. Recalling the words of the Filipino nurse, I say, "Hey, Olan, my smile is hiding behind this mask." He laughs and pulls up a chair.

An hour later everyone departs carrying my plants, flowers, and cards with them. Richard remains behind for a reason. Reporters have contacted him again. They plan to attend the memorial service on Sunday.

"Oh, no, Richard. It must not become a spectacle."

"That's what I told them," he says. "I agreed to see them in your office at the church before the service. But I told them not to talk to you and the girls and not to take pictures during the service. It's the best we can do."

When he leaves, I can't sleep. Again I pray for someone to talk to. The Filipino nurse is not on duty tonight. Soon a Chinese nurse comes in to give me pain medication. I don't want to go to sleep without asking her to pray with me.

"Do you believe in God?" I ask. She looks puzzled. "I need someone to pray with me."

"Yes, I believe in God,"she says, "but I don't have a denomination."

"That's good enough. You just believe and I'll pray." I tell her about the persistence of the reporters and how our grief needs to be respected at the memorial service.

Taking her hands in mine, I pray, not for healing, but for space–sacred space. Amen.

II. Facing Reality

(Spring, 1982)

7

Dust to Dust, Ashes to Ashes

"The Lord giveth and the Lord taketh away;
blessed be the name of the Lord ."
                                                        - Job 1:21 KJV

Saturday, January 9, 1982. At last I'm gong home. I've come a long way in the past five days I've been at Walter Reed. I can transition from bed to wheelchair without help, walk up and down stairs with my crutches, and keep my food down. I'm ready to go home and joke about my skull fracture. "Hey, everybody, you were right. I really am a crackpot." Laughter eases pain.

Mike enters my room with Richard to take me home. I'm glad to see him smiling although his eyes glisten and he still blinks with that childhood nervous tic. I worry about him. How horrible it must have been to see Terry Glen's clothes at the house and the leather-bound chess set on which the boys challenged each other through the years. Terry Glen usually won.

Four days ago Mike turned twenty-five. Ricky will be twenty on the 13th. Tonight we will celebrate their birthdays. Terry and Roger will be missed but we must take this first step toward observing our traditions within our smaller family group.

The nurse wheels me to the elevator, and Mike carries my few hospital supplies in the small pink basin which goes home with me. I claim my egg crate, too.

At the front door of the hospital we find Richard waiting with the VW camper. The middle and back seats have been unfolded to make a bed. Richard and Mike arrange the bedrolls, pillows, and my egg crate for my comfort. Somehow I ease into the camper and lie down to snuggle under the warm comforter. Mike closes the side door and climbs into the front seat. We're on our way.

I don't dare give in to my fears of the traffic, of distant sirens, of possible car trouble. The camper was just recently repaired. A thousand and one "what ifs" tumble through my thoughts as I put pressure on my hip to ease the pain. Someone told me that pain won't kill you, it just makes you wish you were dead.

Mike turns around and smiles. He talks softly. I can't hear. Maybe he isn't talking softly at all. Maybe it's my deafness, the traffic, the engine, my heart pounding. "I'm okay," I assure him. I mouth the letters O-K. He nods and says something to Richard.

Some time later I feel the car leaving Highway 271 at the Clarksburg exit. Richard calls to me over his shoulder. "We're almost home, honey." He pulls up into the driveway, jumps out, and races around to open the sliding door. Mike takes my crutches and Richard lifts me out of the van.

"You can practice with your crutches later. I'm carrying you this time." I don't argue. I just cling to him and pray he doesn't fall on the ice and snow. He doesn't.

Ruth and Joan swing open the front door and I'm truly home at last. I don't know what I expected but I feel overwhelmed by all the voices, blurred faces, the tiny space for so many of us. Richard carries me into our bedroom and lays me on our king size bed. I had hoped to sit up in the living room but I feel exhausted. I tell Richard to invite everyone to come on in. I'm eager to see them.

As my sisters, sons and daughters, and Janice visit me one at a time I hear the vacuum cleaner, the furnace, and Dvorak's New World Symphony playing. That was Roger's favorite. He played the trumpet and french horn in the school band in Germany. Roger paid half the cost of his own trumpet last fall. We paid the rest.

Richard brings Tanya in her wheelchair to me. She seems perfectly composed. Not at all like me, falling apart. We have so much to discuss but I feel inadequate to tell her how fortunate *we* are to have *her* when she has *no* surviving children.

Tanya tells me that Aunt Ruth and Aunt Joan have been taking care of her. "Aunt Ruth slept in Becky's and Paula's day bed last night and Aunt Joan slept on a cot at the foot of my bed. It was like a slumber party," she laughs. "We talked most of the night." I didn't ask where everyone else slept or if they slept at all. As long as Tanya's needs were being met, I knew that all the others would take care of themselves.

The rest of the afternoon I napped. The room was dark when I finally awoke to the aroma of Richard's special beef stew simmering on the stove. Sheilia came into my room. "Mom, supper's almost ready but I wanted to give you something first." She handed me what appeared to be a book wrapped in colorful paper. It's your Christmas gift but it didn't seem appropriate after the accident."

I opened it to find Erma Bombeck's humorous book, *The Grass Is Always Greener Over the Septic Tank.* "Terry Glen and Roger loved this one since they were here when the septic tank backed up," laughed Sheilia. I thought Erma Bombeck would help you take your mind off the accident."

Ruth comes in to help me get up–since I have no trapeze attached to the headboard on my bed to hang on to–and into my wheelchair. "Supper's ready," she announces.

For the first time I get a good view of everyone and everything in the L-shaped living room and dining room. Tanya and I park our wheelchairs near Sheilia as she seats herself on the divan. Everyone else sits around the table in the dining room. We are served on bamboo trays which Sheilia and I purchased in Germany.

I watch Ricky buttering his bread at the table. He is sitting where Terry Glen usually sat. For a brief moment I see Terry

63

Glen's face. The same big brown eyes and medium brown hair like Ricky's, who has now grown to six feet tall like Terry.

"Are you alright, Mom?" Ricky asks.

"I can't see very well without my glasses. It takes a little time for me to focus," I try to explain. Ricky accepts my response and I turn my head to hide the tears.

As soon as the dishes are cleared, Richard and Janice bring in the chocolate birthday cakes singing, "Happy Birthday." Richard joins in singing bass and Aunt Joan sings alto. The rest of us carry the melody. After Mike and Ricky blow out their candles, they open their gifts; shirts and after-shave cologne, books (our family always gives books) and some gag gifts.

While the unwrapping of gifts is in progress my eyes study the corner in the living room where the Christmas tree no longer stands; where gifts had been piled high before we left on Christmas Eve; and where stockings had lain beneath the tree waiting to be filled by Santa.

I wanted everything to be the same as it had been when we left home for church. I wanted to come home and undecorate the tree myself; handle each German hand-painted wooden angel that Becky had held; touch each candy cane that Paula had licked and tossed back into the branches when she got caught; and sniff the scotch pine fragrance of the branches.

Tanya, too, gazes into the empty corner where the Grinch stole our Christmas. Terry Glen delighted in reading the Dr. Seuss book, *The Grinch Who Stole Christmas*, when he was a first grader. But there was no happy ending for him this Christmas. Tanya glances at me with watering eyes.

After the party we go to bed early so we will have strength for tomorrow's memorial service at Westminster. In the dead of night I awake. The winter darkness fills the space like an ancient tomb. It's as though the mourners have carried the light out with them and only the dead remain. The spirits of Terry and Roger seem real. I'm confused. I want to talk to them, to ask them what happened, where they have been. I'm scared. Is it a sin to talk to the dead?

Go away. No, stay. Tell me what to do. Dear God, couldn't you have waited? They're yours for all eternity. They were mine for too short a time. The clanging alarm clock shatters the silence. Richard turns on the lamp and the tomb vanishes.

"We haven't heard from Chuck, he says. Chuck Raymond, a tall black Damascus high school senior, who lives down the road, is Roger's best friend. They rode the school bus together. On week-ends the boys walked down to the pond to watch the ducks and to share stories of their past experiences. Other times they sat on the front porch and talked until the mosquitoes drove them inside. Having moved seven times in his fourteen years Roger was curious to hear what it was like growing up in the same area where you were born.

Roger was disturbed by the Ku Klux Klan forays into our county; the separate churches for black people and for white people; the racial bigotry he had not encountered as an army kid living on post in Germany. He valued Chuck's friendship.

"I think I'll send Mike and Ricky down to Chuck's house and invite him to sit with the family at the funeral," Richard says. "Roger would like that." The boys reported later that Chuck was surprised when they introduced themselves as Roger's brothers. He promised to be ready when they returned to pick him up.

In the meantime Ruth and Joan help Tanya and Sheilia to dress for the memorial service. The girls plan to wear pantsuits which cover their casts. My bangs conceal the lacerations and bumps on my forehead. A slight paralysis of my facial muscles remains. Ruth and Joan apply make-up to give my daughters and me color, so we won't look like we're fading away.

When Richard goes out to warm the rental sedan Mike and Ricky drive down in the yellow Volkswagen camper to pick up Chuck. We had declined the offer of a limousine by the funeral director, Mr. Robert Pritts. Richard has a need to be behind the wheel of the car carrying his wife and daughters. Mr. Pritts understood. He graciously offered his assistance in other ways.

Soon we are led out to the car. I'm not ready for the front seat yet and I choose to sit behind the driver, the position where Tanya had sat when I last drove in December. Joan agrees to ride in front. In the back seat Sheilia slides into the middle, the position in which she was riding, with Paula on her lap, when the accident happened. Ruth slips in beside Sheilia in the roomy sedan. Tanya settles in on the right, where she had intended to ride on Christmas Eve, before Roger got there first. I watch Mike and Janice get into the VW camper. Mike will drive. Ricky, Bob, and Chuck climb in.

Our small caravan leaves Clarksburg and moves over the snow-covered hills toward Westminster. It's the first time the three of us survivors have ridden together since the accident, winding along the same road to the same destination. Silence encapsulates us as our eyes roam the countryside searching for something we have lost.

At Damascus we turn the corner at the gas station where Terry Glen filled our tank in the VW Rabbit station wagon. I wonder if anyone remembers seeing him. Up the street does anyone recall the little blonde-haired girl with her aunt and grandmother at the grocery store where we selected our Christmas tree? We drive on past the water tower at Mount Airy. I look around for a funeral home or morgue where the boys' bodies were taken that fateful day. But I don't ask.

When we reach the crash site, Richard slows down. Skid marks on the pavement and oil stains on the side of the road are the only remaining evidence of our fatal collision. The scene is eerily peaceful. Smoke rises from the chimneys of a cluster of homes. I halfway expect to see Paula riding on Terry's shoulders and Becky tugging at his jacket as he says, "Hey, Mom, you forgot to say good-by." I imagine Roger holding Ruth Ann and singing carols to her. Roger had a clear strong voice and a talent for singing. He was so tender with Ruth Ann when Tanya would place the baby in his arms.

I throw a kiss to my imaginary loved ones. They vanish. Instinctively I look back at the pitched roof farmhouse we just passed and relive that last haunting moment on Christmas Eve before their lives were stolen. I shouldn't have looked back. In my dreams I never get past that spot. But I did look back. I needed to recapture that sense of blessedness when each of us was anticipating our roles in the Christmas Eve pageant.

The remaining ten miles pass without comment. It is fortunate that we cannot read each other's minds. For myself, passing the accident site for the first time is another milestone. We are still alive. What lies ahead will be the sequel.

Entering the picturesque town of Westminster, we drive along Main Street with its refurbished historic buildings until we reach the church. The church is built on sloping ground with the sanctuary on the street level and fellowship hall, classrooms, and a small chapel on the lower level which can be entered directly from the parking lot at the back. We park behind the church hoping to be unobserved. Our protective family help Tanya into her wheelchair and help me to stand securely with my crutches on the bitterly cold pavement. Icicles hang from the eaves. Ice has been cleared from the sidewalks.

Richard leads us inside to the chapel where Karen and Reuben Morningstar are waiting. They will escort us into the sanctuary upstairs after Richard returns from his promised interview with reporters in my office.

"We better take our pain pills now, Mom," Tanya says as she opens her small purse. Sharon leaves and returns with two glasses of water for us. Tanya and I had endured our increasing discomfort without medication as long as we dared in order to take the prescribed dosage just before the memorial service. We didn't know how long we could tolerate sitting up during the service.

When we hear the organ overhead in the sanctuary, Reuben suggests it's time to move toward the chairlift in the hall which will carry Tanya and me up the stairs. The chair lift is a memorial gift to the church from the Morningstar family, honoring Reuben's deceased father, a Methodist minister.

"I think you and Tanya are the first persons to use it," Sharon says.

As I sit down on what seems to be a very small seat I wonder aloud if the lift has an eject button."

Mike winks and says, "No, Mom, it's just the express model."

Thankfully, it is not. My motorized transport steadily ascends to the landing, makes its turns and continues up to the street-level floor. The organ music covers the sounds of our group assembling outside the chancel door. The chairlift returns for Tanya while Bob carries her wheelchair up the stairs. When we are ready, Sharon opens the door to the sanctuary.

Tanya enters first with Bob pushing her wheelchair across the carpeted front aisle. Richard walks beside me as I manage my crutches. I hear gasps and sniffles. The congregation is blurred to my eyes. I take a deep breath and claim the scripture, "The eternal God is thy refuge and underneath are the everlasting arms." I won't break down. I will be strong. I grip my crutches.

From the center aisle I carefully enter the first pew and move down far enough for Richard to sit beside me, leaving the aisle seat for Bob. He parks Tanya in her wheelchair beside the pew. Sheilia enters from the side aisle to sit beside me. She's so thin. Was she that thin before the accident?" Her lip quivers and I reach for her fingers extending beyond her arm cast touching them to reassure her. Next come her Aunt Ruth and Aunt Joan, followed by Janice and Mike. Roger's friend Chuck sits between Mike and Ricky. Like a mother cat looking over her kittens, I must be certain that each of my loved ones is accounted for.

Dr. Edwin Moyer plays the organ arrangement of Ravel's "Pavanne to a Dead Princess" which we had selected as a tribute to Ruth Ann. When I was a student at Wesley Theological Seminary eight years ago I enrolled in Dr. Moyer's class on church music. When I came to be employed by the church he scarcely remembered the student who never stayed around long enough after class to sing in the seminary choir. She always had to dash out to the Washington, D.C. beltway and get home before the school buses unloaded her six children. When I took this job I reviewed my class notes and Dr. Moyer's book, *The Voice of His Praise*, so as not to embarrass my former professor.

The prelude ends and the congregation rises to the notes of the first hymn, "My Faith Looks Up to Thee." Richard doesn't seem surprised when, instead of remaining seated, I ask him to help me stand with the congregation. Steadying myself on my crutches I find that I can see the words about a foot from my face as he holds the hymnal. The words of that nineteenth century hymn, while meaningful to adults, seem inappropriate for children. I wonder how I will manage my grief over our little ones.

After the hymn, Reverend Tom Starnes reads the scriptures. He was our pastor at St. Matthew's United Methodist church in Bowie, Maryland, when Richard was stationed at the Walter Reed Army Institute of Research and I was a student at Wesley Seminary. We appreciated Reverend Starnes' style of preaching during the Viet Nam era when many churches treated military families as persona non gratis.

Dr. Mary Alice Edwards, my former religious education advisor at the seminary, reads from Eugene O'Neill's play, "Our Town." She speaks of God's tears and selects the script in which Emily is allowed to see the effects of her death on her family. Sheilia whispers to me, "We studied that play in school last year. I'm going to memorize those lines." Coincidence? Or did Richard happen to mention that Sheilia was a drama student in Germany?

Dust to Dust, Ashes to Ashes

Reverend Gisselbeck presents the eulogy. He introduces Tanya's children in a real way to those who never knew them. He tells about their baptism during Advent with water from the River Jordan donated by Sheilia. He shares the story of how our toddler Paula always ran, never walked, and sometimes tripped and fell. One morning Paula puckered up to cry after a bad fall, and her big sister Becky sat down beside her putting her arm around Paula. "Here, honey, sit on my lap. You'll be just fine." I hear people chuckling as we, too, look at each other and smile.

This is a good time to sing, "Jesus Loves Me." I know that if there are children at the service they will know this song. Becky's class sang it every Sunday morning. I never noticed the third verse before:

> Jesus loves me! He will stay
>   Close beside me all the way.
> If I love Him when I die,
>   He will take me home on high.

On Christmas Eve when Tanya was dressing her children for the trip to Westminster I had overheard Becky say, "Mommy, I want to see Jesus. I want to see him today." Did Becky learn the third verse? I wondered.

Reverend Gisselbeck chose as the subject of his sermon, "Life's Moments." With Tanya's and Sheilia's permission he shared how they had met their brothers and Tanya's children in near-death experiences moments after the wreck that took their lives. The strange phenomena do not require explanation. Fortunately he offers none.

The chancel seems empty without caskets or easels with pictures of our sons and granddaughters. Maybe it's better that way. They're not here. We must deal with the emptiness left in our lives by their dying without losing the precious memories of their living.

Our spirits now lifted by the children's song of Jesus' love, the service concludes with the affirmation of God's love expressed in the hymn, "O Love That Wilt Not Let Me Go." The stanza, "I give Thee back the life I owe," holds special meaning this side of the grave, for Tanya and Sheilia especially, and for all of us as well.

Following the benediction the congregation depart through the back doors to the sanctuary and the ushers escort us out the side door where Tanya and I will again use the chair lift to descend to the lower level. A reception in Fellowship Hall has been planned so we can thank our friends for their prayers and concern.

At the foot of the stairs I see Karon and Bob Cross, army friends we knew in Germany. "Martha, why is it always you?" Karon cries when she hugs me. Two years ago in Germany Karon prayed by my bedside at the U.S. Army Hospital at Bad Canstadt when I suffered complications following a hysterectomy. Together we had served as officers in the Protestant Women of the Chapel and trained at spiritual life retreats at the Bavarian town of Berchestgaden which Roger thought was the most beautiful place in the world. So did we.

"I jogged seven weeks after surgery, remember?" I reminded Karon. "Pray that I'll jog again."

"Oh, sure, like the song, 'Walking and leaping and praising God,' huh?"

"Why not?" We laughed and wiped our tear-stained faces.

We move on into Fellowship hall and formed a receiving line so our family from Texas and Oklahoma can meet our army family and our new church friends.

"I didn't know you had so many friends in such a short time in Maryland," Michael remarks.

"Where did all these people come from?" Reverend Gisselbeck asks.

"They're our green suit family," Richard proudly says as he introduces army officers and their wives whom we have known at

71

other posts. Like us, many of them are now stationed in the Washington, D.C. area. "We army people are a community wherever we go."

To my pleasant surprise with my crutches I am able to position myself so as not to stress my hip. I can even shake hands. Since my left ear remains deaf I turn my head to listen with my right ear. Faces near me are focused clearly but across the room my blurred vision sees only a crowd resembling an impressionist painting.

Richard tells me reporters are mingling among the visitors and that photographers will be taking candid shots. They kept their promise not to photograph during the service and even now they do not trouble our family for interviews at this time. I appreciate their courtesy.

Kristy Bair brings her six-year-old twins, Jennifer and Carol to me. I'm elated. Kristy had substituted for me on Christmas Eve by directing the children's choir. "You would have been proud of our choir children," she says. "When I gave them your cards and candies that night they thought you had arrived after all. It was hard to explain because we didn't know many details yet."

Jennifer and Carol study my face silently. I can't bend down to hug them but impulsively I lean forward and kiss the tops of their heads. The girls smile. "You can tell the other children that choir practice will start the first week in February," I promise. "Tell everyone that I'll be there." Looking down at my crutches I know that I must toss them soon. I'll need both hands to direct the lively music.

Richard moves about the room introducing our army friends and church friends to each other. Sheilia introduces Mike and Janice, Ricky and Chuck to her classmates who drove over from Damascus with their teachers. We are glad to see Roger's German language teacher and his soccer coach, who undoubtedly know that German was Roger's favorite subject and that soccer was his favorite sport. Ruth and Joan continue their vigil of Tanya in her wheelchair and of me supported by my crutches where we remain in place as the receiving line diminishes.

John Underwood, a civilian from Kelley Barracks who made the pilgrimage to Israel with us last spring, steps forward. He tells how he delayed his return trip from Washington, D.C. to West Germany in order to attend the memorial service. "Prayer groups are meeting all over the place for your family," he assures me.

"Tell them their prayers are being answered," I say and I present him to Tanya whom he had not yet met.

Mary Parker and her son Sean, who was Roger's soccer teammate in Germany, bring us up to date on another mutual friend's grief. "You knew that Richard Nail died of a fast growing cancer, didn't you?" Sean asks.

"Yes, Roger received a call from one of the Graham boys just before we left home on Christmas Eve," I reply.

"Roger was very sad about it when we got into the car," Tanya says. Richard Nail was Roger's age and his older brother Mike Nail was Sheilia's age. Sean's mother tells us more details about Richard's last days. Our shaky voices fumble for words to comprehend the tragedies of young lives lost.

A quiet dark-haired young woman steps forward and clasps my hand introducing herself. Carol Eberhard. I hadn't seen Carol since she and Terry were students in middle school together when we lived in Bowie, Maryland. I wouldn't have recognized her after all these years, nor her younger sister Betty standing behind her. We talk about how she and Terry renewed their friendship in recent years after his stint in Korea and her missionary service in Central America.

"Carol, I thought you might become our daughter-in-law some day. Just because Terry's gone doesn't mean you can't visit us some time."

Suddenly Carol clutches her throat crying, "Terry's dead. I can't believe it." She stumbles back into Betty's arms. What can I say to her? The joy we shared briefly in recounting old memories is suddenly drenched in tears. As I watch Carol and Betty depart holding onto each other, I know that we have seen Carol for the last time.

The crowd disburses and I walk over to the grand piano where Sheilia's classmate Pam Walsh is playing and singing a song she has composed in memory of Roger. While I listen Chuck approaches. "I wanted to stop at your house many times but I didn't know what to say."

"I understand, Chuck. We're glad you came with us today. Roger would have wanted you to be here."

"Roger was like a little brother to me." Chuck and Roger shared a locker at school. Chuck told me his feelings of sadness when he opened their locker and no longer saw Roger's books and green windbreaker stuffed inside. Roger had brought them home for the holidays.

The Fellowhsip Hall is almost empty now except for the floral arrangements which the ushers brought down from the sanctuary. The girls and I select a couple of potted plants and request that the cut flowers be taken to patients at Carroll County hospital. Somehow I forget to have one sent to Reverend Ruth Ross. She is convalescing at home from her surgery and I miss her terribly. I'll phone her tonight.

Reverend Gisselbeck escorts us through the hallway to the back parking lot. The chill wind blows through the legs of my pantsuit. The boots which Tanya and I usually wore to protect our legs against the winter cold, disappeared from our feet the day of the accident. Maybe they were too badly damaged to be returned to us. Cautiously, Tanya and I lower ourselves into the back seat again with Ruth and Joan in the middle. Richard and Bob pack the crutches and wheelchair into the trunk.

Richard inspects all the tires and discovers that the left front tire is nearly flat. He turns on the key and drives to the nearest service station to use the air pump and check the air pressure on the other tires. I feel sorry for him trying to take care of all of us. First

74

the broken water pump at the house and now the flat tire after the memorial service.

As we leave the service station, I look up into the colorless sky. It's as though an opaque dome seals the quiet town in wintery gray. I feel like a zombie in one of the science fiction plots Terry Glen liked to read. Stark leafless trees, silhouetted in the early twilight, protrude out of icy snow banks like firewood ready to be gathered. No signs of wildlife peer out at us. No signs of life at all.

Too soon our tragic locale appears over the hill on the inward curve. It catches me by surprise. Pain shoots through my hip as we drive over the oil-stained spot where innocent lives were crushed. I stiffen and bite my lip. Time stands still.

We pass in silence.

8

Cabin Fever

"But they that wait upon the Lord shall renew their strength;
they shall mount up with wings as eagles; they shall run,
and not be weary; and they shall walk, and not faint."
- Deuteronomy 40:31 KJV

Before Mike and Ricky return to Texas I want them to sort through Terry and Roger's belongings together and take those things which they wish to keep. If I go downstairs with them to their brothers' basement room they will defer to me. They need to do this project without me.

Tanya asks Mike to help her down the stairs. The heavy cast on her leg is hard to manage. "Aren't you coming, Sheilia?" she asks.

"Tanya, are you sure you want to go down there?" Sheilia frowns.

Neither of the girls has been down to the basement since the accident. The play area for Tanya's children is located around the corner from the foot of the stairs on a red rug. Tanya had set up a toy box, small shelves with story books and puzzles, and a Walt Disney castle with a pink dragon and fairyland characters. Roger had donated the castle and Terry Glen had donated the rug which we purchased the year Sheilia was born. Red was Terry's favorite color. After he joined the army Roger used the rug in Germany. It still wore well after all these years.

"I thought about the basement a lot in the hospital, " Tanya replies. "We have to face it sometime"

With tight lips, Sheilia hesitates and glances at me. "If you want to wait, honey, you can wait,"I say. She tells Mike and Tanya to go on down. Mike helps Tanya start down the first step. The oldest brother and oldest sister are still leading the way for their siblings. Ricky follows.

Sheilia has a good excuse for not joining her brothers and sisters tonight. Captain Frank Hiller, a Medical Service Corps officer formerly on Richard's staff in Germany, arrived today from Fort Sam Houston, Texas. His plane arrived too late for the memorial service but not too late to accept our invitation to dinner at our home. Sheilia was glad to see him again and only wished that Roger had been here also.

"Did your cuckoo clocks ship without damage?" Frank asks Sheilia. Before we left Stuttgart, Roger had voiced concern about the way the packers were boxing up the clocks we had purchased for him and his sister.

"Yes, they did." Sheilia answers. "Mine still tells time and Roger's still predicts the weather." On Roger's clock a figure of a girl wearing the traditional full skirted German dirndl rotates out of a chalet in sunny weather and a boy wearing lederhausen knee britches circles out in rainy weather. "We see more of the girl in Maryland than we did in Germany," Sheilia laughs.

Captain Hiller had met Terry Glen in 1978 when our son visited us at Kelley Barracks, West Germany, shortly before Christmas. Terry Glen had stayed long enough to help us decorate the Christmas tree and secure the angel on top, but his leave had not extended to Christmas.

Now we listen while Captain Hiller tells us how our army family learned so quickly about the accident. The VII Corps Army commander Lieutenant General Julius W. Becton, II, whose headquarters were at Kelley Barracks when Richard served on his staff as corps surgeon, had spread the word of our tragedy.

The general and his wife Louise were currently living at Fort Monroe, Virginia. Mrs. Becton had mentored me through the intricacies of military protocol and army regulations when I was elected president of the Officers' Wives Club at Kelley Barracks. She had a knack for recruiting persons to roles which utilized their talents and enhanced their opportunities for growth. A registered nurse, Mrs. Becton could be empathetic without coddling.

Captain Hiller now had orders to be stationed at Fort Monroe. "Frank, why don't you let Martha and me drive you down to Fort Monroe tomorrow instead of flying? We can thank the general in person and it will do Martha good to see Mrs. Becton again."

I'm as shocked as Captain Hiller who looks directly at me. Would the doctors at Walter Reed allow me to extend my pass another day? Would I be able to lie down and sleep most of the way? I sure couldn't sit up that long. My pain medication should help.

When the boys and Tanya come back upstairs, they're surprised to learn of the sudden change in plans. Bob will drive Ricky, Mike, and Janice to the airport in the morning for their return flight to Texas. Aunt Ruth and Aunt Joan will stay with Tanya and Sheilia. If the doctors agree–and Richard thinks they will–we can make the round trip in one day.

"Well, Mom, you never did stay down long, did you?" teases Sheilia. She should know. She took her first flight on military orders when she was three days old. I was stranded in Houston awaiting the birth of my fifth child when Richard was commissioned a captain in the medical corps at William Beaumont Army Medical Center in El Paso, Texas.

Aunt Ruth and Uncle Ken were babysitting our brood of children–Mike, Terry, Tanya, and Ricky–at their ranch near Ada, Oklahoma, where the Ken Lance sports Arena was projected to open in August. While riding herd on our lively bunch for three weeks (baby Sheilia was overdue) Ruth and Ken were also preparing to host their first big rodeo, an enterprise which lasted thirty years.

Hours before I was scheduled to catch a flight to El Paso to join Richard I went into labor. Richard obtained an emergency leave and arrived in Houston before our daughter was born. In the meantime the army notified him that our household belongings had arrived in El Paso and he must return to claim them.

With my three-day-old baby in my arms I rode with Richard to the airport studying a map he handed me and trying to grasp what he was saying. "Welcome to army life, Sweetheart. I'm on standby in military uniform to save money. Therefore I could get bumped if the seats are filled by paying passengers. If I do, here's a map to the house I rented and here are the house keys and car keys. Our car is parked in lot . . . ." I never heard where the car was parked. I had already made up my mind that if he didn't get on that plane with me and my baby, I would phone William Beaumont Army Medical Center upon my arrival to send someone for me. Thankfully, the three of us boarded the plane together. The next morning Ruth was on the first flight with the rest of our children, who couldn't understand why we needed another baby. After all we had Ricky.

Snapping out of my brief reverie, I answered Sheilia. "No, honey, I don't stay down long, thanks to your dad and his sudden ideas."

The next morning finds us on our merry way to Norfolk, Virginia, after Richard promised the doctors he would bring me back to Walter Reed for a check-up later in the week. Cushioned in the back seat with pillows, comforters, and my trusty egg crate, I hibernate like a bear, waking only once for a bathroom stop. Soon we cross the bridge into Fort Monroe and leave Captain Hiller at the bachelor quarters. Along the seawall we locate General Becton's quarters among the two-story historic red brick houses on Generals' Row. Fortress Monroe, as it was originally named, is located on a strategic point of land overlooking the Chesapeake Bay. The oldest fort in our nation's history, it is also the only military post with a moat surrounding the original casement walls.

We park in front of General Becton's quarters and I count the twelve concrete steps up to the porch. Richard hauls out my crutches and I begin my trek. Halfway up the steps I hear the front door open and Mrs. Becton's voice calling, "Martha Proctor, what do you think you are doing?"

"Climbing Jacob's ladder?" I reply.

"Julius is not going to believe this when I tell him. He's out of town right now and he'll be sorry he missed this sight." We all breathe a sigh of relief when I cross the porch without mishap.

After an hour's visit we start home, revived by the social call and refreshed by coffee and cookies. The five-hour drive home seems shorter to me than the trip down to Norfolk. When we reach Gaithersburg, eight miles from home, we stop at Pearle Vision to select new frames for my prescription lenses. Looking in the mirror, I notice that the slight paralysis of my face is less visible. Slowly my face is returning to its normal appearance.

When we get home, Sheilia hands her dad a list of phone calls from persons who attended the memorial service. "They wanted to know if we needed anything and I told them we were doing just fine," she said. Her first day back at Damascus High School was not as intimidating as she had expected. The teachers were kind and her classmates carried her books.

A course in the history of Maryland was required for high school graduation. Therefore it was the one subject in which Sheilia and Roger enrolled together. She sat behind him in class. "I thought Roger's empty seat would be hard for me to take," she tells us. "I cried every night for the past two weeks just thinking about it. I guess that helped. By the time I got to class, I had talked to so many friends that I almost forgot about it."

Sheilia has a lot of homework to do to make up for the days she was absent. But she needs it to divert her thoughts from our tragedy and help her to return to a stable life. She and Roger were good students.

Ricky, Mike, and Janice are probably home in Texas by now. Bob said their flight left on time. I hadn't been able to talk to the boys as much as I had wanted. I didn't know how to help them cope. I'm glad that Mike had Janice here with him. We didn't get to know her very well before we left for Germany. Janice was a godsend to us during this sad time. She coordinated meals and kept a list of the food people brought so their dishes could be returned and we could send thank you notes. Janice was the invisible helper behind the scenes taking care of details that never crossed my mind.

Tuesday morning, Richard leaves early for his office at the Uniformed Services University of Health Sciences in Bethesda. The faculty and students are planning a memorial service scheduled for tomorrow morning. Richard has a backlog of work to handle.

He left so quickly I didn't realize he wasn't coming back into our bedroom. I look around for something to help me pull myself up to a sitting position. Nothing is handy. I hear the school bus stopping across the street to pick up students. Sheilia will board it. I pray that whoever helped Sheilia to dress for school this morning will peak in on me too.

God must get tired of my praying for every little thing but nothing is a little thing to me right now in this condition. The Bible says to pray without ceasing. Doesn't that mean incessantly? Somewhere I read that the unconscious prays when the conscious can't. Maybe that's what dreams and nightmares are–unconscious prayers all mixed up. *Please, Lord, help me to sort it all out but first help me to get up.*

Ruth pokes her head in the door and whispers, "Martha June, are you awake? How about a cup of hot tea?"

"Thank goodness you came in, Ruth. I need you to hang on to so I can get out of bed. Let's drink our tea in the living room."

Soon we are comfortably ensconced in our afghans on the divan sipping lemon herbal tea. The heavy mug warms my freezing hands as early morning darkness isolates us like campers in a tent.

"Mother wants you to call her today," Ruth tells me. "Since Mother and Daddy couldn't fly back here for the memorial service their pastor conducted a memorial service in McAlester at at the same time we were attending ours at Westminster." I feel guilty that I had totally forgotten about them at that hour. In fact I scarcely remembered our phone conversations when I was still in the hospital. It seems so long ago.

"Mother said that three pink rosebuds on the altar for Becky, Paula, and Ruth Ann opened and bloomed during Reverend Storey's sermon." *Thank you, Lord.*

Ruth tells me how Ken broke the news to Mother and Daddy on Christmas morning. "Ken and I arranged to meet Joan and Olan in the parking lot at Tandytown Shopping Center at McAlester so we could drive to the house together. Mother was surprised to see both cars arrive at the same time but she didn't suspect anything. Ken said, 'Mom, Dad, we have some bad news. We better sit down.' Mother and Daddy sat down in their recliners. Joan and Olan gathered around Mother, and Ken and I gathered around Daddy."

Closing my eyes to stiffle the tears I can see my folks sitting on the edge of their Lazy-Boy recliners. All our childhood they tried to protect us from death by never taking us to a funeral, not even to Aunt Lou's funeral. Aunt Lou was my dad's favorite aunt who paid the country doctor when I was born on Granny's farm.

"Ken told them, " Ruth continued, "that you were okay before he told them who had died. Without a word Mother fumbled with her corsage of pine cones and bells until she got it off and laid it on the end table. She started screaming. Daddy started sobbing. When Mother heard Daddy crying she stopped screaming and went over to him. He kept repeating that Mike and Terry Boy were dead. Finally we got him to understand that Mike was alive but Terry and Roger were dead."

Ruth talks fast like a TV commentator. "Mother phoned Reverend Storey and he called the church members who came to the house. Her neighbor across the street brought over her own Christmas dinner. She said her group was coming later and she could fix more. Mother cancelled our reservations for the Holiday Inn Christmas buffet. We waited all day to hear from Richard. Ken told Mother that we should phone the hospital. Mother was relieved when she heard your voice."

I want to know more but apparently we have awakened Tanya and Joan. We hear them talking. Then Joan sleepily comes out and tells Ruth that she will fix breakfast if Ruth will take care of Tanya. Ruth dries her tears and clears her throat before going to Tanya's room. Bob comes in from the den where he has slept all night and turns on the TV to hear the news. More accidents, more crime, more stormy weather.

Soon Tanya joins us in her wheelchair. Ruth and Joan bring our breakfast trays set with fried eggs, whole wheat toast and grape jelly, and hot chocolate with miniature marshmallows. I don't feel like eating but I know I must. Bob cuts Tanya's eggs for her into bite-size pieces and puts a straw in her hot chocolate. She can't hold a mug with her arms and hands encased in casts to her fingertips.

"Mom, I saved Roger's blue soccer shirt for Sheilia," Tanya says. "I thought she would want it since she went to his soccer games in Germany. Mike and Ricky divided Terry's silk shirts that Granny made for him when he was a teenager."

Tanya says that her brothers gave Terry's flannel shirts to her and Sheilia to wear with their jeans. The boys didn't feel that they could bear to wear his clothes. The colorful silk shirts, however, were a precious keepsake of Granny's memory as much as a keepsake of Terry's life.

Throughout the dreary day I'm lost in a fog of hazy thoughts trying to connect people, places, and happenings. Merciless pain holds captive my mind, my voice, my body. How can I go on never seeing my sons again? Will I go crazy? Some grieving mothers do.

Will I become bitter like my great-grandmother did when her husband died? She, too, had lost a son who died from tuberculosis.

Dear God, help me. I don't want to be crazy. I want the hurting to stop. I want to comfort my family. Please, please, Lord, protect us from any more harm.

Later in the day Ruth and I go downstairs to the basement. In the boys' room their unopened Christmas gifts tied with ribbons and bows lay stacked on their beds. I'll have to open them later but not today. Terry Glen's scuffed brown loafers peer out from underneath the hem of the bedspread on the floor.

Ruth calls to me from the laundry room. "Martha June, the hospital returned this sack of your clothes to Richard." She brings me the brown paper bag and I pull out my blood-stained ecru blouse trimmed with lace on the collar and cuffs. "All that blood was yours?" she gasps.

"Or was some of it Terry Glen's?" I wonder aloud. "Throw it away, Ruth. I could never wear it again, even if we were able to get the stains out." I feel suddenly faint. "Let's go back upstairs. I need to lie down."

Hobbling on my crutches I cross the basement to the stairway. Ruth pauses to look at the children's play corner. She shares memories of the red rug from Terry Glen's childhood, his Dr. Seuss books, and the hopes that Joan and I had shared that our granddaughters would grow up together.

Joan's oldest daughter Lorri had a baby girl only three months older than Tanya's Becky. We had taken photos of our daughters and their babies when Becky was nine months old and Lorri's baby Freedom was nearly one year. That was the only time the infant cousins ever met. Freedom wasn't impressed with her younger cousin when Aunt Tanya handed Becky to Lorri and picked up Freedom to play with her. If only the children could have known each other as three-year-olds last month. They would have had a lot of fun together.

Ruth and I go on upstairs where Joan is playing the piano for Tanya. Joan had listened for the phone while Ruth and I were in the basement but there were no calls. I'm glad that my sisters are able to stay with me my first week home. It would have been so lonely for Tanya and me with Richard at work and Sheilia in school.

Wednesday, January 13. Ricky's twentieth birthday. I'm glad we celebrated his and Mike's birthdays last Saturday before they left for Texas. This morning we prepare to attend the memorial service for our sons and granddaughters at the United Services University of Health Sciences (USUHS) in Bethesda, Maryland. It was kind of the faculty and students to do this but I feel a bit nervous. I scarcely know anyone at the school. I hope I won't cry in public. Tanya won't cry. She has already steeled herself not to cry except when she is alone. Sheilia however will need extra kleenex in her purse. She always cries when someone is suffering. Bless her heart. She misses Roger so much.

Ruth, Joan, and I ride with Richard this morning in the rental sedan while Bob drives Tanya and Sheilia in the Volkswagen camper. Snow flurries drape the world in white during the thirty-mile trip to Bethesda. Arriving at USUHS we descend into the parking garage beneath the school. At least I won't have to manage my crutches on ice and snow. A young officer approaches and escorts us inside and up to the auditorium. We move along at a fast pace. Bob pushes Tanya's wheelchair and I hobble along as quickly as I can. Waiting at the entrance for us a young woman lieutenant ushers us in to the open front row before the students assemble.

When the medical students appear I'm impressed with how good they look wearing their military uniforms. First and second year students are commissioned as second lieutenants in their branch of military service. Third-year students are then promoted to first lieutenant and upon graduation the fourth year they will be promoted to captain and receive their orders. Several officers stop to speak to Richard and to convey their condolences to me before the service begins. I feel the sadness I've been suppressing ever since the day I came home from the hospital. A few tears leak out but overall I hold up fairly well.

Joan whispers something to me but she is sitting on my left side and my left ear is totally deaf. I point to my ear and she understands. Tears trickle down her face and she reaches over and pats my hand.

This time we will not be able to avoid the reporters who have arranged with Richard to interview us in his office after the service. Fortunately the men are not intrusive in their questioning and do not detain us long. We agree to a photo shot. Then Richard accompanies them out of the office still in conversation. When he returns he takes one look at his in-box and asks me if I could stay a little longer with him while Bob takes my sisters and our daughters home. "Or you can go with them, if you would rather."

Without hesitation I decide to stay. I'd rather be here with him than home without him. Shortly after the others leave I notice snow piling up on the windowsill. It hasn't stopped snowing since we left home this morning. In less than an hour an officer notifies us that everyone else is leaving because the storm is worsening. Richard stacks some papers into his briefcase and locks up his office. This time I move briskly on my crutches as we hurry to the parking garage which is almost empty.

Richard opens the car door for me and takes my crutches which he tosses onto the back seat. Quickly he turns on the key and drives out into the slow moving traffic. The radio announcer reports which roads are already closed. I hope our family isn't stalled somewhere. We creep along until we are reach our exit for highway 271 north. Listening to the news we hear that Air Florida flight 109 departing from Washington D.C.'s National Airport has plunged into the Potomac River. I shudder at the thought of lives which will be lost in the freezing waters. As horrible as our own tragedy is, I realize that our family will not be the only one which suffers death this winter. We listen to the rescue efforts being made and hope they will be successful but it doesn't sound good.

When we take our exit to Clarksburg we find the two-lane road covered with snow except for tire tracks. Fortunately our home is only one mile from the exit. We see our VW camper parked off the side of the road and are relieved to know that our family reached home safely. In our driveway our neighbor is operating his snowplow shoving snow off to the sides. What an unexpected blessing. He waves a gloved hand as he moves on down the slope and crosses the road into his own driveway.

Inside the house we find everyone gathered around the TV watching the rescue efforts on the Potomac. A woman reaches for an inner tube. Chunks of ice float around her. How frightening it must be clinging to life knowing that you have only minutes to be rescued.

"Ruth," I exclaim. "You must cancel your flight right now. We've had too many deaths in this family already."

I need not have worried. Tanya had already convinced her. The remainder of the week we follow the progress of the five crash survivors in the papers and on TV. Planes were de-iced and the weather finally improved. Flights resumed more or less on schedule.

Over the week-end Ruth returned to Oklahoma. Bob stayed to be with Tanya. Joan prepared to stay with me as long as she was needed. The week had been a trial of endurance for all of us and it wasn't over yet. Tomorrow our church would host a public forum on the issue of drunk driving. I absolutely must attend.

9

Forum: Drunk Driving–a Dead End

"There is a way which seemeth right unto a man,
but the end thereof are the ways of death."
- Proverbs 14:12 KJV

Sunday, January 17, 1982. Icy roads. If I didn't feel that I needed to be present at the public forum for the sake of Terry Glen and Roger I wouldn't venture out of the house today. Richard will go anyway but I need to go with him. Like the proverbial mailman, neither rain, nor snow, nor heat or cold will keep my husband from his duty. As for me I now find the winter roads intimidating.

Inside our home shadows of our five missing loved ones lurk behind bedroom doors, empty chairs, and the draperies covering the bay window where Paula loved to hide. Echoes of their voices call out to me from every room. I hesitate to leave Tanya and Sheilia here even though Bob and their Aunt Joan will be with them. But I can do more good by accompanying Richard to the forum.

Promising them that we will drive safely we set out over the Maryland hills for Westminster. Gray clouds as dingy as the slushy snow on the road darken this dismal hour. When we approach the accident site I dare not take my eyes off the tire tracks of the vehicles ahead of us. It has only been a week since the memorial service but it seems so long ago.

Arriving at the church we find the parking lot full and cars parked on the street for some distance. The handicapped parking space however stands vacant and we believe that I qualify for that space today. So we park.

The low, wide steps at the front entrance are manageable for me with my crutches. As soon as we enter the foyer a middle-aged couple step forward and tell us that their church is praying for our family. Their radiant faces contrast with the somber expressions of others in the crowd. Dr. Moyer overhears us talking to the couple and turns around with a big smile.

"Martha, I didn't expect to see you here." He extends his hand to Richard. "Both of you look much better than you did last week." I'm glad to hear that. Someone finds Reverend Gisselbeck who quickly briefs us on the agenda for the evening. He hadn't expected us either but expressed his pleasure that we were able to come. As he ushers us to a pew I ask him to seat us on the left side of the sanctuary, but not on the front row, so I can hear the speakers with my right ear. Someone calls him away after we are seated.

What a change has taken place in the sanctuary converting it from a house of worship to a public meeting house. Reporters and photographers dash around stringing electrical cords, testing lights and microphones. Men begin to cluster around a speakers' table in front of the altar railing. A woman with a mike in her hand approaches Richard, speaks briefly, and turns to me lowering her microphone as though to speak "off the record."

"I know that you don't want to talk to me, but do you agree with your husband's statement?" Not knowing whether she is recording and my being unable to hear what Richard said I reply simply. "We believe that drunk driving is a societal problem and we hope that stronger laws and better educational efforts will result from today's meeting. If that happens our children will not have died in vain."

She says that our accident has made her stop and think about her own drinking. She favors the designated driver as a sensible alternative. "Yes," I remark, "if you can find someone who will forgo drinking for the evening." I have my doubts since drinking alcoholic beverages is an addictive habit.

The microphone on the speaker's podium squeaks loudly and after corrective adjustments have been made, Reverend Gisselbeck opens the meeting. He welcomes the crowd and states the purpose of the forum to address the issue of drunk driving in the state of Maryland. Before he introduces the panel of speakers he asks everyone to stand who has lost a loved one to a drunk driver. As Richard and I rise, I'm amazed and saddened to see so many others also standing. We stare at one another with the pathos of fellow sufferers who know, that even now as we assemble, our numbers are being increased by fatal alcohol-related accidents somewhere else.

I sit down trembling at the thought that possibly survivors never heal. Are we condemned to a life sentence of melancholy, half-alive and half-dead? On the one hand I'm grateful for the concerned citizens here today but on the other hand I'm grieved that it is our family's tragedy which has galvanized them to action, not for the first time but once more. How many will have to die before people will take responsibility for their own drinking habits and not get behind the wheel of a car?

We listen to heartbreaking accounts of others who have been through this ordeal of grief. Mothers Against Drunk Drivers (MADD) is well represented. We learn that the daughter of Candy Lightner, founder of MADD, was killed only last year on her way to school by a drunk driver who lost control of his vehicle. Don Sexton, president of Maryland's chapter of MADD, relates the account of his son's death last July which prompted him and his wife to join MADD when the defendant received only a $200.00 fine. Carroll County, where our accident happened, does not have a MADD chapter yet.

The statistics are overwhelming. Nearly twice as many arrests for driving under the influence were made in Maryland in 1981 as in 1980, yet by December 1 the death toll had already climbed to 420 persons compared to 471 the previous year. Democratic legislators, Senator Paul Sarbanes and Congressman Michael Barnes, introduced bills in Congress this year for stricter legislation. Representatives from the Maryland Governor's Task Force on the Drinking Driver cite recently passed legislation with results too early to assess properly. Spokesmen from Montgomery County and Prince George's County task forces on drunk drivers present the magnitude of the problem which is exacerbated by "slap on the wrist" court sentences. MADD is concentrating its efforts on the courtroom and trial outcomes.

CBS on "Sixty Minutes" and ABC on "ABC News Nightline" provoked national interest when they aired special programs New Year's Eve on drunk driving. We aren't the only ones who heard from people who saw Sam Donaldson's interview with Richard. Many citizens wrote to their Congressmen for government action. President Ronald Reagan is forming a "Blue Ribbon" panel to investigate the issue and propose solutions.

A package of six recommendations for tougher laws will be presented to the Maryland state legislature. It is apparent that the Governor's task force, the county task forces, MADD chapters, and other citizens' organizations have done their homework. But legislation alone won't stop the carnage. Attitudes must change and scapegoats don't change society's attitudes. We don't want to see the defendant in our case made a scapegoat whose conviction and sentencing will assuage a few consciences but change nothing. We must go beyond that and work to change attitudes through public education on the physiological effects of alcohol consumption on the driver, personal responsibility, and alternative choices.

My head throbs as I strain to hear. Fortunately Richard takes good notes and I will question him later. For now my body can't handle any more violence, verbally or physically. I ache to return home as my stamina ebbs away. Realizing that I can't live my life trapped in rage I am determined to fully recover but I will need time and privacy with my own family.

At the close of the forum we leave with mixed feelings of hope for the legislation sponsored and of despair at the unfathomable situation confronting us. Nearly halfway home a shrill siren electrifies every nerve in my body. Richard pulls off the road as an ambulance flashing its red lights speeds past us. Up ahead we see red flares sparkling against the snow. Police stop the traffic and vehicles line up behind us their headlights blinding us in our rearview mirror. My pulse races and I can't stop crying. We wait, praying silently, until the police clear the road and motion the line of traffic past the accident. A few miles later we encounter a similar scene but the traffic is not detained as long. When we reach Damascus I feel safe. We're almost home to Clarksburg.

As soon as we enter the house Joan warms up some chicken noodle soup for us. Richard and Bob discuss the outcome of the meeting while the rest of us listen. Joan washes the dishes and Sheilia reports that just about all of our relatives phoned today. Tanya and Sheilia had a busy but pleasant day after all.

We go to bed early so Sheilia will have a good night's rest before going to school tomorrow and Richard will be ready to tackle his schedule at USUHS in the morning. My head sinks into my pillow and sleep takes over quickly but in the night grotesque images invade my dreams.

"NO! NO! NO! You CAN'T take him." I struggle to scream but only monstrous sounds escape my constricted throat.

"Martha, wake up. You're having a nightmare. Wake up."

Twisting my head erratically, my heart pounding, I force my eyes to open. Slowly my voice returns. "Richard, they were trying to take you away. Creatures, gory creatures were grabbing you. They said they were going to kill you."

"Honey, it was only a nightmare. I'm right here and I'm okay."

"I thought I could stop them if I screamed loud enough. They had sensitive ears and my screams would scare them away. I wouldn't turn loose of you."

92

"Well, I'm glad for that. You just keep holding on to me and I'll keep holding on to you. Okay? Richard hugs me and I feel safe.

Please, Lord, don't let anything happen to him. I love him, and our daughters need both of their parents.

10

Life Goes On

'To everything there is a season . . . a time to weep,
and a time to laugh: a time to mourn, and a time to
dance."

Ecclesiastes 3:1. 4 KJV

January 26, 1982. Good news. Tanya's bones are knitting
more quickly than anticipated. Today's x-rays confirmed it when
the cast was removed from her left arm, but the steel plate
implanted in her right arm necessitates her wearing that cast a while
longer. Now she can write again. Tanya, a lefthander like Roger,
the grandfathers, and me, writes on her calendar for the first time
since the accident.

The doctor has assured me that I can start walking a few
steps without my crutches with no risk of anatomical damage. It's
only a matter of how much pain I can bear. Tanya suggests that I
try walking around her wheelchair. She engages her brake so if I
suddenly need to hold on to her chair I can do so safely. Handing
my crutches to her I extend my hands, palms down for balance, and
scoot one foot slightly ahead of the other, hobbling like a robot in
low gear, until I grab the wheelchair and beg for my crutches.

Over the next several days I attempt this exercise until I am
able to circle the chair with more cheers than groans. Tanya soon
announces, "Next time, Mom, when I give you back your crutches

you can throw them across the room. Tanya's a good cheerleader. By the end of the week we celebrate my progress and hers by gathering around the fireplace in the breeze way instead of the hearth in the living room. Richard suggested that we needed the change of atmosphere for our fireside evenings to mark the turning point in Tanya's and my recovery.

The glassed-in breezeway connects the house and garage and provides the stairway to the basement. A door opens to the front yard and another door faces the woods beyond our back yard and the small red brick storage barn by the fence. This room serves as our library and an office for Richard. Bookcases line the brick walls. His old metal Sears executive-style desk is located beneath the front window panels offering a pleasant view of the countryside over the housetops across the street below. I remember the day Richard's new desk was delivered to our home when he was a medical student at Baylor School of Medicine in Houston. Mike was three years old. Our youngster clapped his hands and ran to tell us that "Mikey's and Daddy's desk is here." In time his dad bought a desk for Mike and another one for Terry Glen.

In our wheelchairs and rockers the four of us settle down to warm ourselves by the roaring fire in the brown stone fireplace listening to soft music Richard plays on the old stereo. Our family seems so small since five of our members are no longer living. Moistened eyes gleam in the light of the sparkling flames and we huddle closer to each other.

Suddenly the storm door rattles. Our faces turn and wait for whom we know cannot appear. Terry Glen and Roger should be coming in from building a snowman like they did last month. But it is only the north wind banging the storm door. We look at each other and turn back towards the fire. The moment is almost sacred. We speak of the boys and the babies as though they were still with us. Perhaps it would help us to release them to the past if we held on to them in the present a little longer until each of us is able to let go. Yet in a spiritual sense they will always be with us.

"I'm so glad we have both of our daughters," my husband whispers when we retire for the night.

The next morning after Richard drove off to work and Sheilia boarded the school bus, I hobbled into the den to choose a book to read. Tanya must be sleeping late and I didn't want to disturb her by listening to the TV.

"Will somebody help me?" I heard Tanya's voice calling from the basement. Had she fallen and lain there waiting until help came? Hanging on to the bannister, I hurried down as fast as I could limp and found her sitting on the bottom step.

"I thought you were asleep. How long have you been down here?"

"Not long. I didn't want to bother anyone so I sat down on the top step and scooted down here to Becky and Paula's play corner. I wanted to be alone and thought I could pull myself back up the stairs again." She rubbed her right arm. "But my arm just couldn't take it."

"Oh, honey, I would have helped you if I had known. Do you need boxes to pack the toys in?" She shook her head. It was too soon for that. She missed her children and it broke my heart to watch her trying to retrieve a sense of their presence. Her little ones should have been playing with their Christmas dolls on the red rug and having a tea party with us.

Leaning on each other we trudge back up the stairs to Tanya's room. There on her bed lay three small dolls which Aunt Ruth had sent to Becky, Paula, and her namesake, Ruth Ann. The dolls were attired in crocheted dresses of variegated colors and matching bonnets. After Christmas Tanya had unwrapped the dolls while Aunt Ruth was still here. Together they cried and shared their grief over the little sisters who never saw the dolls they would have treasured.

The gloomy day drags on as we watch icicles lengthen where they hang from the eaves. Church was cancelled last Sunday due to the ice storms and if the bad weather continues we won't go next Sunday even if worship service aren't cancelled. We close the draperies to save the heat in our poorly insulated home.

In the afternoon a knock on the front door surprises us. We hear the school bus starting up again after it unloaded its passengers in front of our house. "Roger's home," Tanya instinctively announces, as she had done so often in the past. Becky and Paula liked to run to their Uncle Roger and grab his trumpet case. With his arms usually filled with books he was only too happy to let them drag his trumpet case inside.

"I'm sorry, Mom," she says when she realizes her mistake. With tears streaming down my cheeks I open the door to find Tanya's physical therapist. We had forgotten that she was coming today for her first home visit. Apologizing for my crying I excuse myself and leave Tanya with her visitor. Looking out my bedroom window I see that Sheilia is still talking with other students who live nearby. Before the physical therapist finishes the exercise session with Tanya she makes a note to arrive earlier in the day next time.

Tanya seems refreshed by her visit. So refreshed in fact that now she is ready to dismantle her children's day bed. She engages Sheilia and me to help her rearrange her room after we take the children's bed to the garage. By the end of the week Tanya has sorted through the boxes of her children's clothes which Aunt Linda had packed at her request while Tanya was in the hospital. She selects a few dresses to give away and repacks the rest.

With her left hand freed from the rigid casts she begins to journal. In subsequent days she completes the girls' baby books with their pictures, notes, memorial service bulletins and sympathy cards. She slips the 8x10 photo of Becky and Paul back into its frame from which it was taken when she asked her dad to bring it to her in the hospital and tape it to the window by her hospital bed. Now she will hang the picture on the wall in her room.

While working on these projects she never cries. I'm concerned. She talks of recurring nightmares in which she tries to save her babies. She says her arms ache to hold Ruth Ann, to reach around Paula and Becky, to hug them close. She sleeps with the fuzzy Bugs Bunny that Aunt Linda gave her and asks if that's strange. I reason that a temporary surrogate, whether it be a soft pillow or a stuffed toy, is healthy for a convalescing young mother, recently bereft of her babies and still confined to a wheelchair and walker. I predict that she will no longer need the comforting bunny when the cast comes off her leg.

Tanya has only one picture of Ruth Ann. It was taken Thanksgiving when she was five days old. We gathered at the table with Becky sitting on Sheilia's lap and Paula on mine. Terry Glen and Roger sat opposite each other, and Richard snapped the camera. We had forgotten about it until Richard developed the roll in January. Then we realized that everyone in the picture had been a victim of the accident–five fatalities, three casualties. The roll of film contained other snapshots related to the accident–our smashed vehicle and oil stains on the pavement where the accident occurred.

But thankfully someone else had taken a picture of Ruth Ann. Steve Shipley, teacher of the fifth graders in Sunday School, had brought his camera to church the Sunday that Tanya and Ruth Ann portrayed Mary and baby Jesus for the children's department. Steve phoned us one evening and brought his wife Annette and her parents to visit us in our home. He presented Tanya and me with our own copies framed and matted. Best of all baby Ruth Ann was looking up at her mommy's face.

Tanya nearly leaped out of her wheelchair with joy. Later she would hang Ruth Ann's picture on the wall beside Becky and Paula's picture. Somehow it was significant that Thanksgiving and Christmas marked the beginning and ending of Ruth Ann's brief time with us.

Sunday, January 31st. At last the wintery weather abated and we were able to travel to Westminster for church services again. Kirsty Bair phoned yesterday and asked that I meet with her in the church library during Sunday School so she could update me on the children's ministry. Even though I could walk at home without my crutches I used them this morning so I wouldn't be jostled off balance in the crowded hallways. My joints still ache too much to bear my full weight for an extended period of time.

"Would you like to go downstairs to the chapel?" Kristy asked. The children's classrooms were located on that floor and I was eager to look in on them again. When we reached the chapel however I saw boys and girls assembled in the pews.

"Oh, Kristy, they must be holding a special service. Let's not disturb them. We can go back to the library."

"Look again, Martha," she beamed. "Those boys and girls are your choir. They're expecting you."

A boy looked back and saw us. "There she is. There's Mrs. Proctor," he exclaimed. Heads turned and the children whispered excitedly. Kristy and I entered and walked down the center aisle. One girl reached out and touched me. A boy asked, "Are we going to have choir practice, Tuesday?"

"Not this Tuesday," I answered. "But we will definitely start rehearsals the next week. I just saw the music this morning for our spring musical. But I need time to look it over. I know you're going to like it."

"We sang real good on Christmas Eve," another boy said with pride. Heads bobbed up and down in agreement and smiling faces looked up at me. The children's enthusiasm was delightful and I hoped that my deaf ear would recover its hearing before next week.

A brown-haired girl handed me a bouquet of calico fabric daisies with green pipe cleaner stems. A tall boy held up a large poster displaying the children's artwork and writings signed by each child. Among the handwritten cards I received from the children while I was in the hospital one particularly touched my heart: 'We went into the choir room today and cried." This morning their crying and mine was over.

Tuesday, February 2ⁿᵈ. Richard agreed to drive me to work my first two days back on the job. We left early so he could circle back to Bethesda from Westminster. He would return in the late afternoon to pick me up.

It was 7:00 a.m. when we parked at the curb in front of the church. Richard unlocked the glass paneled door to the education wing and handed me my key. Once inside I locked the outside door and waved good-by with a kiss as I watched him drive off. No one else would be here this early and I welcomed my solitude because I knew exactly what I intended to do. I would retrace my steps through the Journey to Bethlehem rooms which I last saw on December 23ʳᵈ before I turned off the lights and drove home.

A glance around my office revealed that it had been left untouched. The brass Middle Eastern lamps I had brought for the Wise Men's tableau and the early American oil lamps for the social time in Fellowship Hall remained in their boxes. Why had no one used the props? Did they feel they were intruding? At least Kristy had distributed the small tins of candy and the Christmas cards which I had personalized for each child.

"You even wrote a different message for Jennifer and for Carol," Kristy had told me at the memorial serivce. "Most people don't, since the girls are identical twins." I remembered asking Kristy to help me to know Jennifer and Carol as individuals. One was slightly taller, the other a little shyer. I had watched and identified slight differences until I could call each girl by her own name.

Leaving my office I began my pilgrimage down the hallways. First stop was the Young Adult classroom where the Annunciation had been portrayed by two young pregnant women in the roles of Mary and her cousin Elizabeth who was pregnant with her baby John the Baptist.

Next was the Senior High classroom. I wondered where Roger would have knelt in the shadow play of the shepherds. The third station was the Inn where a harried innkeep would have been running around trying to find space for everyone. We had a lot of fun planning that scene.

Up the stairs at the end of the hall I passed a sign, "Sh-h-h. Baby Sleeping." The sign was still posted because this floor is seldom used. Stopping at the Stable however I found that the hay, blankets, and improvised stable shed were gone. For a few minutes I imaged Terry Glen standing beside Tanya as she tenderly rocked her tiny baby in her arms. I wondered how he might have felt playing this role.

Sheilia had planned to wait "back stage" in the adjoining room that night prepared to fill in for Tanya with Becky's new doll wrapped in a receiving blanket. I had given the doll to Becky for her third birthday in November. Ironically the doll suffered a fate similar to Ruth Ann's. We read in the newspaper that Ruth Ann's head was crushed against the dashboard when she was catapulted from her mother's arms on impact with the other vehicle.

After the accident Tanya had wanted to pack the doll away with the other toys. But when it was returned in a sack, she opened the bag and recoiled in horror. Sunken eyes, partially hidden by a wisp of blood stained hair, stared out from a fractured head. "Take it away," she screamed. "Get rid of it."

Shivering at these recollections I groped my way back to my office and collapsed at my desk to rest. After the stable scene the Wise Men would have pointed the travelers to Fellowship Hall for refreshments, punch, and caroling. But Kristy said that wasn't the way it happened. People had clustered in small groups waiting to hear more details about our accident. When the ministers did not return from the hospitals the families finally left.

Kristy had told me that the phone rang in the church office as she was locking the doors. Grabbing a pen she answered the phone and began to write in a shaky hand. She said she couldn't believe the names of the dead. When she hung up she broke down and cried. Then she took the list across the street to the parsonage where Helen Gisselbeck awaited her husband's return from the shock trauma unit in Baltimore.

Noises upstairs interrupted my thoughts as other staff members arrived. Since my car wasn't parked outside no one knew that I was here. Quickly I placed several small gifts in a basket and headed for the stairs. My favorite Filipino basket had been splintered in the accident but the gifts which Roger had wrapped were not damaged.

When I entered the church office, Dixie, the church secretary exclaimed, "What are you doing here so early?" She hugged me, wiping away her sudden tears. Then taking the basket I handed to her she set it on her desk. Hearing our voices Reverend Gisselbeck came out of his office wearing a quizzical smile. I explained that Richard brought me and that I had walked through the Journey to Bethlehem stations and that I was glad to be back at work and . . . .

They stared at me in disbelief. "We planned to go with you downstairs to your office this morning," Reverend Gisselbeck said. "We thought it would be easier on you." Touched by their thoughtfulness but fearful of pity I quickly changed the subject and offered my gifts; sachet angels, colorful glass ornaments, a drummer boy plaque, and a leather embossed key ring.

Somehow I got through the day. On my bulletin board I tacked up the poster which the children gave me last Sunday. The calico daisies brightened the winter day when I located a green vase in which to arrange them. Placing the vase on the small table beneath the poster I thought they looked as sweet as the children who made them. I put up a calendar for the new year and sat down at my desk to work out a rehearsal schedule for the rest of February and the spring. The day passed more quickly than I had expected and if it weren't for my notes I probably would have remembered very little of it by the time Richard picked me up after work to take me home.

Throughout February it was difficult for me to leave Tanya alone each day but she made it perfectly clear that she had had enough sympathy. To appease me she agreed to invite a neighbor over for coffee in the afternoons. In the mornings she wanted to be alone to meditate and to journal. One day I noted on her calendar the words, "Cried for Becky today."

After I started to drive again in March Tanya phoned Dixie at the church office one morning. "My mom isn't feeling well. Be kind to her today." Upon my arrival at the church Dixie smiled and asked, "Who is pampering whom? Hm?" I felt embarrassed. When I got home I learned that Tanya also had phoned her dad at work "to cheer him up." Her unexpected call pepped up both of them. After that he looked forward to her afternoon calls.

Spring emerged from its winter dormancy and people continued to show their concern for Tanya's well being. Friends from the Young Adult class drove out to visit her. Her teacher of the short course she took at Montgomery Community College last fall invited her out to lunch while Tanya was still using her walker. That was another turning point for Tanya.

She managed her walker quite well even though her right arm was elevated on a special platform which her physical therapist designed to support the weight of the cast. Weeks later when the leg cast was removed and Tanya could again walk without crutches, a neighbor invited her to walk over to her house down the street for a home Bible study with other young mothers.

My hip continued to strengthen but in the bitter cold it ached miserably. I often shifted my weight while sitting trying to find a more comfortable position. It was much easier to stand or to walk than to sit. Maybe I needed to read and write standing at a podium instead of sitting at a desk. Getting out of a car I had to unbend my joints slowly like an old woman. During my lunch hour, if the sidewalks were not icy, I took short walks to limber my joints and restore my circulation.

Driving past the accident site on my way to and from Westminster I often wondered about the people living in the homes nearby. I wanted to knock on their doors and ask questions; to thank those who phoned for emergency assistance and those who used their fire extinguishers to cool the smoking engines. Caution constrained me. At the preliminary hearing in Westminster the trial date had been set for April and I dared not do anything that could adversely affect the proceedings for either the state or the defendant. Perhaps these people had been advised likewise.

One day I parked at the side of the road and just sat in my car. The vacant frontage was as bare of vegetation as a new grave. A phrase tormented me. "You left me by the road today." Not until its meaning revealed itself in a poem which I struggled to write did I find closure.

Immortal Son

You left me by the road today.
　　You left without good-by.
The others promised they would tell
　　Just how you chanced to die.

They said they heard you call my name.
　　If I had answered, Son,
You would have stayed, I know you would.
　　Death should have been undone.

Dear Son, my injuries forbade
　　My hearing and my knowing
The blood that covered you and me
　　Announced your life was going.

I dare not hear the others grieve.
　　I seek your form and face.
In shades of night, I hear your breath,
　　Feel closeness in this place.

Life Goes On

Stay with me, Son, and help me through
   This pain that grips my soul.
I hurt to breathe, I choke to cry,
   Blurred vision takes its toll.

You left me by the road today.
   I listen for your voice.
I'll write you into life again.
   With God we shall rejoice.

God had set my pen in motion to open the tomb and see the angel of hope. The resurrection promise of spring had come at last.

✧ 11

On Stage

"And we know that all things work together for good
to them that love God."

- Romans 8:28 KJV

Tanya had a need to be needed. She turned her attention to
her young sister. In early December the girls had read an article in
the *Damascus Courier* which interested Sheilia.   The Miss
Frederick Beauty Pageant would be held in the spring and
rehearsals would begin in February. The winner of the competition
would compete for the Miss Maryland crown who would represent
the state in the nationally advertised Miss America pageant. Sheilia
had decided to enter the contest and do a jazz routine in the talent
category. But the accident changed her life. She participated in no
extra curricular activities at school. After her morning classes she
went to her job at the National Bureau of Standards. At home she
spent a great deal of time alone in her room doing homework and
dropping off to sleep from fatigue.

"Tanya, I couldn't possibly enter the contest now. What
would they think if I showed up for registration with my arms in
casts? They would think I was crazy."

"You're not going to dance on your hands, Sheilia. The
casts are coming off soon anyway. Your jazz routine is really great
and there's still time to take a few dancing lessons to polish it off.
I'll help you with rehearsals." The self-appointed cheerleader knew

her sister had talent and Tanya was determined to see her use it and move on with her life.

"Maybe you're right, Tanya. When I auditioned for my first school play Mom said it doesn't matter whether you win or lose it's how you apply that experience. I didn't get the role for which I auditioned, but I got the right role for me, and I was on stage during most of the performance. You could say I had a front row seat," she laughed. Sheilia had a way of finding the humor in stressful situations.

Having convinced herself that she could do it her next hurdle was to convince the committee. She phoned the contest sponsors for directions to the sign-up location, scheduled weekly private lessons with a local dance instructor, and unpacked her leotards. Tanya put the music tape in the cassette player and settled back in her wheelchair to appraise Sheilia's first rehearsal on the smooth hardwood floor in the basement. Closing her eyes Sheilia listened to the jazz beat absorbing the rhythm until her feet carried her out into a nonstop dance. It was a painful first try but an encouraging one nonetheless.

Tanya even accompanied Sheilia to her dance lessons so she could learn how to coach her rehearsals at home. Both girls were still wearing their casts at the time Richard and I drove them to Frederick for the orientation. We waited in the parking lot while the girls registered. Each contestant was assigned a hostess who would help her to shop for an appropriate wardrobe, accompany her to her interviews, and assist her backstage with costume changes. Six weeks of rehearsals would begin next week.

When the girls returned to the car they bubbled over telling us all the details. "When the director saw my casts she questioned whether I would be able to perform so soon. I told her that would be no problem because the casts were coming off this week. I didn't mention the accident and she didn't ask. I don't think she recognized my name and I was glad."

"I knew when Sheilia got in there," Tanya chimed in, "that

she would be inspired. When they started talking costumes, styles, and swimsuits, Sheilia was hooked."

The girls sailed through the next six weeks with excitement and a bit of apprehension. Richard noticed an elegant white ball gown in a store window in Bethesda the day before the pageant. "It's perfect for Sheilia," he insisted. The next morning we took her to the store. When she walked out of the fitting room and whirled around in front of the full mirror, there was no doubt that the gown was made for her. We couldn't really afford it after all the medical bills but that didn't matter. She deserved it. A trip to the hair stylist completed the transformation of our Cinderella. She was ready to go to the ball.

But first she must dress for a personal interview with the judges. The selection process had begun. Now it was time for Tanya to step aside along with the other "stage mothers." The assigned hostesses would take over and see their charges through their interviews and all other portions of the competition. We wished our daughter good luck and kissed her good-by. Then we went home to dress for the long awaited evening.

Sitting in the audience at the theater later that evening, I felt like we were normal human beings again. Tanya's leg cast had been removed several weeks earlier and she didn't even limp. My facial paralysis was gone and Richard's color had returned. We were immensely proud of our daughters for their courage tonight.

Backstage the contestants would be lining up for their dramatic entrance and introductions before the individual events would begin. We hoped Sheilia would not draw number one. Her nervous parents believed she needed to be farther back in the line when the seventeen lovely hopefuls marched out for their first appearance. The lights dimmed, music played, and the curtains rose. The audience stood and clapped as the gorgeous young models entered the spotlight and paraded down the walkway. The master of ceremonies clearly introduced each contestant by name, town, age, and her school or place of employment.

At last he announced number twelve and Sheilia appeared. To our astonishment she had drawn Roger's athletic number. Walking briskly down the runway like a young woman who knew where she was going she radiated joy and beauty. I could hardly hold back the tears. Sheilia maintained confidence throughout the swimsuit competition, the street clothes judging, and the talent performance. When she modeled the white ball gown in the final event, she looked as happy as a child playing dress up. At age seventeen she was indeed the youngest contestant.

"Ladies and gentlemen," the Master of Ceremonies paused. "The third runner-up is Miss Sheilia Renée Proctor of Damascus High School." Tanya and Richard were already standing in the aisle, cameras flashing, when Sheilia walked across the stage to receive her trophy, a smaller replica of the Miss America trophy. I clapped and cried and hugged Tanya, then Richard, and clapped some more.

Sheilia's triumph took me back to her first school play when she was chosen for the role of the youngest Von Trapp child in "Sound of Music." She had only two lines to say, two times, but she was on stage throughout most of the play. It was just right for her at that age and she was ecstatic. Yes, third runner-up was just right for Sheilia tonight and she looked so happy.

Photographers posed Miss Frederick and her court for camera shots. The proud *Damascus Courier* photographer snapped a picture of Sheilia as her dad planted a kiss on her cheek. Afterwards we joined the other young models and their families for a reception. One of the judges told us that if Sheilia continued her dancing lessons she could go to the top in a couple of years. She had that kind of poise. The judge encouraged her to consider it.

A man turned to Tanya and suggested that she should enter the "Miss Teenage America" contest. Obviously pleased that he thought she was the younger sister, Tanya replied, "Thank you for the compliment but I'm twenty-one."

On the way home Sheilia talked about her surprise at

drawing the number twelve. "I could hear Roger saying, 'Take my number, Sis, and run with it.' " That is just what Roger would have said if he had been here tonight. He and Sheilia were always there for each other.

"Did you ever think that playing dress-up when you were a three-year-old would pay off when you were seventeen?" I asked. Of course I was speaking of the time when Richard was stationed at Kagnew Station, in Asmara, Ethiopia. Richard and I came home from the commissary and five-year-old Ricky ran to meet us. Three-year-old Sheilia trailed behind him wearing my old blue formal and trying not to trip as she gathered up the sides of the voluminous skirt. Frowning at her brother she admonished him. "Ricky, you don't leave your princess on a picnic."

At home we finished the roll of film taking pictures of our winner and her "stage mother." At last our sleepy Cinderella stumbled into bed. "Sweet dreams, Sis," Roger would have said. It would be her first joyful night's sleep since Christmas Eve.

Our daughters' successful achievement in preparing Sheilia for the Miss Frederick pageant was a welcome diversion from the impending trial which was repeatedly delayed throughout the spring. The defendant had been charged with five counts of vehicular homicide and five counts of automobile manslaughter. He cannot be convicted of both. The former carries a sentence of two years per count while manslaughter carries a sentence of three years. Additional charges of driving under the influence, failure to keep to the right, and reckless driving are made.

We had hoped to get the trial behind us before Sheilia graduated in May and went off to college at Oklahoma State University. Richard had been selected shortly before our accident to attend the next class at the U.S. Army War College at Carlisle Barracks, Pennsylvania, in July. Future general officers and their staff would be selected from the graduates.

We're into the Lenten season now. At Westminster the choir mothers fit the children in blue robes with white ascots.

When the choir rehearses with Dr. Moyer at the organ I'm very pleased with the way the children deport themselves. We will sing one anthem during Lent, another on Palm Sunday, and one on Easter. The remaining weeks we will devote to rehearsing our spring musical, "Moses and the Freedom Fanatics" by Hal Hopson.

Sunny weather blesses Easter morning and the church is packed to overflowing. Dr. Moyer plays the organ introducing the first hymn at full volume. The congregation rise to their feet and the choirs begin the procession from the foyer down the aisles singing as they march. Visions of Becky and Paula in crisp Easter dresses and lacy stockings flash through my mind. My watery eyes stare at the open hymnal in my hands as I lead the children's choir up into our rows in the choir loft.

I dare not catch anyone's eye for fear of weeping. For the children's sake I must not cry. They're watching me for their cues. As we continue to stand singing the last verse I look into their happy faces and smile. A couple of children whisper and wave to their families in the congregation. Parents and grandparents, aunts and uncles, and cousins are here today. I give the children my most pleasant "eyes forward" look and they respond with grins dropping their hands quickly to their sides their long sleeves almost covering their wiggling hands.

When we are seated after the "Amen" I focus my gaze on the red carpet. I dare not look at Reverend Ruth Ross who I know is praying for me. If I do I will cry. From the pultpit Reverend Gisselbeck says the pastoral prayer and I take a deep breathe. *Please keep praying for me, Ruth.*

The children stand to sing our anthem and I pull myself together. As they sing the last stanza Dr. Moyer and I exchange pleased looks. He nods his approval to the children. Kristy and I escort our charges out the side door and around the corner to the choir room where they will hang up their robes. When we slip into the sanctuary again, it is so crowded that we can't help all the children find their parents so we take them to the library. There we

111

can listen to the Easter service over the public address system. At the reading table an eight-year-old child looks at one of the Bible story booklets donated by Grace Lutheran Church in memory of my sons and grandchildren.

"I didn't know that your sons died," she says. "I knew you were hit by a car. You were in the hospital a long time."

How do you talk to a child about death? I try to answer her questions and hope I say the right things. She changes the conversation to her new puppy. "Maybe your mother can bring your puppy to choir practice so all of us can see him. Puppies are cute, aren't they?"

During the singing of the doxology Kristy and I take the children to the foyer to await their families when the ushers open the sanctuary doors. Richard, Tanya, and Sheilia are waiting for me. My family looks tired. Tanya holds a pot of lilies which Becky's Sunday School teachers donated for this morning's service in memory of Becky. It is the custom on Easter and Christmas to fill the chancel area with flowers contributed in memory of loved ones.

As we drive home, Tanya comments on the purple iris, red tulips, and yellow daffodils blooming in the small communities through which we drive. Nature's colors appear brighter than usual this spring after the long bitter winter. I once read that "Faith is believing that under the snow, the flowers of springtime patiently grow."

"Our daffodils haven't bloomed yet," Tanya remarks, "like the flowers of our neighbors across the street." Last fall Tanya and Roger dug out the brick enclosed front flower bed beneath the master bedroom window. They planted countless daffodil bulbs while I played with Becky and Paula. As we pull up into the driveway at home, Tanya is the first to notice that her daffodils have opened their buds. "I've been watching every day and they weren't blooming when we left for church this morning," she says.

"Roger planted his own memorial," Richard observes. Two

weeks later another happening, likewise foreshadowed, occurred when the puppy of the young choir child was killed by a car. During the next choir practice the children prayed for her and for her puppy. She thanked me afterwards for talking to her in the library about death.

May 9th. Mother's Day. Aunt Ruth's birthday. Tomorrow is Paula's birthday. She would have been two. Paula had so much personality she didn't know what to do with it. She left her tiny hand prints on a bookshelf in the library before the paint was dry. Sometimes I lay my hand over the precious imprint and talk to Paula in my thoughts.

Tanya won't be going with us to church today. She will spend the day with friends. Church is the last place she wants to be on Mother's Day since she has been robbed of her motherhood. She needs time apart. Later in the day I phone Mother but the long distances lines are busy all day in our area and I'm not able to reach her. It's the first time I haven't talked with her on Mother's Day except for the years we were stationed overseas. Mike and Ricky each phoned me last night to tell me they would be thinking of me on this special but sad day.

Our lives become more complex as the end of the school year approaches and the trial date again has been delayed. The lawyers are having problems finding qualified jurors. In the meantime Richard and I drive up to Carlisle Barracks for our briefings by Colonel Darrell Powell, president of the graduating class, and his wife Alicia. As the ranking member of the new class in July Richard will be president of the sixteen seminar groups and I will have duties coordinating activities and projects with the wives of the seminar leaders. Our five-hour briefing leaves Richard feeling exhilarated and me overwhelmed. Fortunately Alicia has prepared thorough after-action reports and a complete calendar of events. On the way home we discuss how much we enjoyed the Powells' hospitality and hope we will look as good at the end of our year at the U.S. Army War College as they do.

Sheilia brings home Roger's high school annual. His picture is bordered in black, labeled "In Memoriam." I want to give his classmates a chance to sign his annual but decide against it. Maybe that would be too morbid. I find myself doing what I think Roger would be doing at this time–tossing out old schedules of soccer and football games and collecting newspaper clippings about school functions for his scrapbook.

I display Roger's and Sheilia's school pictures in matching frames. Sheilia looks radiant in her cap and gown. Her fellow workers at National Bureau of Standards give her a dictionary for college, some fun gifts, and a book of firsthand accounts of near death experiences. The stories disturb her. She treasures her own spiritual communication with Roger moments after the accident but is uncomfortable sharing it with others.

On graduation day Tanya and I sit in the stands at the stadium while Richard wanders around taking candid photos for Sheilia. The boys wear green robes and green mortar boards while the girls wear white. The school colors are obviously green and white. When the band strikes up its marching music I close my eyes and see Roger at another time, another place–a year ago in Germany–wearing his band uniform and blowing his trumpet. I find solace in such memories but sometimes the unexpected flashbacks trigger my tears. After the ceremony we find Chuck and congratulate him on his graduation.

We have another graduation to attend–that of the young lieutenants at USUHS. However rain is predicted and before the ceremony starts in the courtyard of the university the crowd is forced to move their chairs under the arches at the sign of the first sprinkling of raindrops.

Mrs. Betty Koop, accompanied by a woman wearing the rank of Vice Admiral in the Public Health Service, sits next to me. Mrs. Koop's husband, Admiral C. Everett Koop, newly appointed Surgeon General of the United States, is the commencement speaker. We soon find that we share a mutual sorrow, the death of

114

a son. The Koops' son fell to his death on a mountain climbing trek a few years ago. She promises to give me an autographed copy of their book, *Sometimes Mountains Move*, which relates their experience in learning what happened and how they coped with their grief.

The last item on our calendar of events for May will be the children's musical at Westminster United Methodist Church. It has been six years since a children's musical was performed in this church. On Sunday, May 23rd the balcony is filled and we run out of programs. "People must think it's Easter or Christmas," comments one lady. The chancel has been transformed into Pharoah's great house with Egyptian pillars created by the Senior High class under the supervision of their teacher, Bill Pond.

Kristy and the choir mothers costume the children in biblical-style clothes including sandals. Frog dancers in black leotards and paper mache frogheads hop around gleefully. Senior High students play the roles of Pharoah, Moses, his brother Aaron, and his sister Miriam.

When I sit down at the piano to play the opening march, I wonder what I'm doing here. *I can't see* (my trifocals were a problem), *I can't hear* (only partial hearing has returned to my left ear)*, and I've never directed a musical before* (a detail I overlooked until now). Placing my hands above the piano keys and breathing a quick prayer, I come down forcefully on the opening chords of the introduction and beat out the steady rhythm of the chant, "Listen, King Pharoah, We Want Freedom."

Moses leads the band of Israelites charging down the aisle carrying placards, shaking rattles, and thumping their tambourines. Pharoah appears and Moses threatens while Miriam and Aaron try to advise their brother. The Israelite slaves sing and dance to a Middle Eastern beat. Moses calls down the plague of frogs which croak, "Ribbit, Ribbit, Ribbit" leaping and croaking every where.

Forty minutes later Pharoah gives up. A jubilant parade of freed Israelites follow Moses out of Egypt (back up the aisle) singing Alleluia that they are free at last. Then they sing the doxology, "Shalom." Peace.

"Mom, why didn't you tell me it was going to be so good?" Sheilia squeals as she descends the stairs from the balcony with Tanya and Richard behind her. "If I'd known it was going to be that great a production I would have been willing to help you with the choreography, costumes, and dress rehearsal. I thought it was just going to be a few songs like a program.

Following the performance the choir mothers and I had planned a luncheon in Fellowship Hall. Unknown to me however the ministers and Kristy had coordinated a church-wide farewell potluck in my honor. Kristy gave me a cloth-bound journal in which to journal. "You have such good ideas," she said. "Write what comes to you in this." It was too lovely in which to record my confused feelings and meandering hopes. But I did begin to journal in a spiral notebook after that.

I returned one more time on Pentecost Sunday to assist with the confirmation of the sixth grade students whose six-week class of instruction I had co-taught with Reverend Gisselbeck. Reverend Ruth Ross would confirm the youth since Reverend Gisselbeck and his wife Helen had been granted the opportunity to celebrate Pentecost in Israel this Sunday.

"We didn't think you would be back," said one of the girls as she hugged me.

"Did you think I would miss your confirmation?" I asked. "I wouldn't miss something as important as that."

After the service I noticed a tall, middle-aged man standing behind the wheelchair of an elderly woman. "She wants to talk to you. Her eighteen-year-old grandson was killed last year by a drunk driver. The boy had spent part of his last summer with her."

The lady reminded me of my own Granny. Terry Glen had loved her so much that he spent part of his army leave time visiting her in Oklahoma. Fourteen months before his death, Terry Glen had attended Granny's funeral. This lady must have been such a beloved grandmother. She spoke with warm affection of her grandson. At a loss for words I leaned over and kissed her. That is what Terry Glen would have done.

Granny (Vera Fay Huchel) preparing breakfast on Thanksgiving, 1960, three months before a drunk driver crippled her for the last nineteen years of her life.

III. From Golgotha to Bethlehem

(Summer to Winter, 1982)

Twelve Days That Never Were

"Cast thy burden upon the Lord and he shall sustain thee."
- Psalm 55:22 KVJ

July 7, 1982. Traveling along the scenic eastern shore of the Chesapeake Bay in our new Mercury station wagon we listen to the news on the radio. Richard is expecting an announcement. For nearly a week he has been sworn to secrecy. The trial, originally scheduled for April, will start tomorrow but the location has not been made public. A change of venue was granted after sufficient jurors who were not acquainted with any member of our family or the account of the accident could be found in Carroll County where the crash occurred.

"Easton, Maryland," announces the radio commentator. The trial has been moved to Talbot County and is expected to last five to seven days. Tanya, Sheilia, and I have been subpoenaed as witnesses for the state. Tom Hickman, state's attorney, does not plan to put Richard on the witness stand.

"I don't think I can go through this," Sheilia says. It was painful enough for her when she made her statement in the office of the prosecuting attorney in Westminster. "I looked up and saw him (the other driver) coming in our lane," she had said. "I wasn't afraid. I thought Mom would get us out of it. She always had."

"Honey, we have to do it for Terry Glen and Roger, and for Becky, Paula, and Ruth Ann. Their voices can't be heard except

121

through us," I remind her. I almost feel like Terry Glen is depending on me to testify for him.

Sheilia looks out the window at the sunlit waters of the Chesapeake Bay. "I can do it for Roger." Her voice breaks. "He would have done it for me."

Arriving at Easton we check into the motel where we were told to meet state's attorney Tom Hickman. We go to our rooms prepared to stay until tomorrow morning when a police escort will take all the prosecution witnesses to the court house. Until then we must avoid conversation with other persons except Richard's brother Terry who has arrived from Houston and Tanya's ex-husband Bob Jeanette who has returned from Alabama to watch the trial.

The next morning at the appointed time a state trooper knocks on our door. In the parking lot a line of official vehicles is forming with their passengers. Tanya, Sheilia, and I ride together. Our driver parks in front of the old stone court house and all witnesses are escorted into the court room. The defendant sits at a table with his attorneys who thumb through papers in their hands. His wife sits with his mother and his aunt in the first row back of him.

The bailiff calls the people to rise and the presiding judge enters. The judge steps up to his chair behind the judicial bench and gives permission to be seated. Throats clear nervously in the court room. Then all witnesses are asked to stand and identify themselves. Still standing we are clearly instructed in the rules of sequestering. The defense attorneys request that witnesses for the defendant be sequestered separately. Permission is granted. All witnesses are escorted from the court room and that is the last we see of the courtroom today.

The room to which we are taken is bare of all comfort. The chairs at the long wooden table where we are seated are neither padded nor furnished with cushions. A law enforcement officer monitors our conversation and a guard is posted outside the door.

A glance around the room finds only bare walls. No rug, pictures, bookcases, cabinets, draperies, lamps, or water fountain furnish this interior. The witnesses look at each other without comment. At least we are not prohibited from gazing out the tall locked windows where I see a pair of sparrows disappear into the leafy branches of a tree.

The hours pass and no one is summoned. The guard steps in and talks briefly to the law enforcement officer but nothing is communicated to us who wait. At noon we are told that court has been adjourned for lunch and we may dine with our families at the restaurant of our choice. Again we are cautioned to discuss nothing about the morning's proceedings. Our families have been advised likewise.

Richard takes us to the Golden Corral. Witnesses for the defense have come as a group to the same restaurant so we choose a table far away from them. After a light salad buffet the girls and I are refreshed enough to face the afternoon at the courthouse. Richard, Bob, and Terry return to the court room.

Only one witness is called from our group during the first hour. Finally one woman says she doesn't like being forced to take sides. The law enforcement officer looks at me and says nothing. I respond that it isn't a matter of taking sides but of telling the truth of what she saw and heard.

Pushing my chair back from the table I tell the officer that my bones ache too much to sit on this hard chair any longer and that I am going to walk around the room for exercise. He remains expressionless. Tanya and Sheilia look at me with faint smiles. "Come one, girls. It's okay. I know that you need the exercise too." They stand up and Tanya massages her sore knee.

I walk over to the windows and look out above the treetops to the clear blue sky. When I was a child I drew pictures of castles in the clouds. If I sketched a castle today I would draw the dungeon spiraling down into a huge dark thundercloud.

When I turn around Tanya and Sheilia are pacing laps the

length of the room. Soon everyone is stretching, moving around, and talking about the weather. Really, what else can we talk about? One by one the other witnesses are called. Only one returns and she says nothing.

Every day is like this the rest of the week. All the witnesses are called except Tanya, Sheilia, and myself. Court is adjourned for the week-end. What's going on? Still under the rules of sequestering the girls and I may not read, hear, or watch the news until the trial is over. Prohibited from discussing the proceedings with us, Richard, Terry, and Bob look glum and tight-lipped when they come for us after court is adjourned.

Leaving Terry and Bob at Clarksburg, Richard drives the girls and me on to Carlisle where our household goods were shipped just last week. Neighbors bring over covered dishes of food. Richard explains to them why the girls and I cannot talk about the trial. They acquaint us with the history of Corey Apartments which used to be a dormitory for Indian girls when the Indian Industrial School was established here in the late 1800s. The ghost of an Indian chief's daughter who died in a dormitory fire is said to roam the five apartments. She was last heard in our apartment. Her remains are buried in the small cemetery on the grounds of Carlisle Barracks.

Monday morning we return to Easton. Tanya says frankly, "I will NOT go back in that empty room." Richard finds a breezy walk through near the court room and speaks to the prosecuting attorney about it. The judge grants permission for the girls and me to wait there under the vigilance of a law enforcement officer. Again we are not summoned to testify.

When we return to our motel at the end of the day the girls and I express our feelings that we are being treated more like prisoners than witnesses. Again Richard talks to Mr. Hickman who says that the girls will probably testify tomorrow morning and I will probably be called in the afternoon. Therefore I may stay in my room at the motel for the morning. As it turns out only Sheilia is summoned. Tanya must return with me after lunch to the court house.

"Sheilia wasn't on the witness stand very long," Tanya says.

"I didn't have much to say," Sheilia explains. "They could see that I was about to cry."

After lunch we leave Sheilia at the motel where I grab Richard's small Bible from the bedside table. Surely no one will mind if I read the Bible while I'm waiting. As we wait in our familiar niche at the court house Tanya looks up one of the Psalms. She has scarcely finished reading it when the bailiff comes for her. "Take it with you," I say, when she offers the pocket-sized Bible to me.

"Thanks, Mom." Unlike Sheilia, Tanya is composed and ready to walk into that court room. She knows that I will be praying for her throughout the questioning. When the bailiff returns for me some time later Tanya slips the palm-sized Bible into my hand as we pass.

In the court room I am questioned and cross-examined for nearly an hour. Only once does my voice falter. In re-living the moments preceding the collision I see the windshield covered with snow crystals and I hear Terry Glen call, "Mom." But I knew there were no snow crystals on the windshield. In that instant my voice trembles. The judge calls for a five-minute recess and orders the bailiff to bring me a glass of water.

Regaining my self-control I tell the judge I am prepared to resume the session. *These people want to hear what I have to say. I will say it in my own words at my own pace and not be rushed or harassed by the defense lawyers.*

At times they seem to be trying to put words in my mouth. I refuse to bite. When they repeat my response tagged with their own phrases I simply repeat my exact words until I am quoted verbatim. I am asked to draw a sketch depicting the location of each vehicle. I advise the court that I am not an artist and cannot draw perspective. With that understanding I attempt to draw the requested sketch. When I erase, the defense lawyer objects.

"May I remind the court that I am not an artist and I cannot draw perspective." The judge acknowledges my statement and I erase my pencil marks and redraw my sketch on the flip chart mounted on the standing easel.

I am shown a series of photographs taken by a police photographer. The pictures retrace the approach to the accident site. I am instructed to walk before the jurors and identify the photos to each juror. First I caution them that these views are not the views from the driver's seat. I study the last photo intently–the oil stain on the pavement.

At the close of my testimony the state's attorney requests permission for me to remain in the courtroom with my family. The defense lawyer jumps to his feet. "We might have reason to recall this witness later in the trial." Therefore he objects.

"Your Honor, I am more than a witness. I am a victim."

The judge nevertheless rejects my request and reminds me that I am still under oath and under the rules of sequestering. I suspect that the lawyers do not want the jury reading my face for reactions to their strategy during the remainder of the trial.

Returning to our motel at the end of the day I tell Richard what caused my voice to falter in the courtroom. "I heard Terry Glen's voice. He reached for my arm. Then I saw snow crystals on the windshield. But I know there wasn't any snow on the windshield, Richard."

"It was shattered safety glass," he explains. "The cracks would resemble snowflakes when you looked at the windshield from the inside."

"Mom, Terry Glen did reach for your arm." Tanya goes on to say that "The last word he said was 'Mom' but he barely whispered it. He didn't sound scared." So my experience was confirmed and that gave me some relief.

Richard, Terry, and Bob attend the trial daily. The girls and I stay at the motel. Each day that the trial plods on our enforced sequestering becomes more unbearable. Sheilia needs to go on out to Oklahoma and get settled for her freshman year at Oklahoma State University. Once more the judge is entreated on our behalf by the state's attorney. After consultation with the defense lawyers the judge grants permission for the girls and me to leave the state, still under oath and the rules of sequestering. We must submit names, phone numbers, and addresses where we can be reached should our return be deemed necessary.

Friday night we return to Carlisle Barracks and by early Saturday morning the VW camper is packed tightly with Sheilia's college gear and her beloved German shepherd Rex. Bob will drive us straight through from Virginia to Oklahoma. Terry will stay with Richard. "I'll phone you as soon as the trial is over," Richard promises.

Traveling through the Blue Ridge Mountains of Virginia I feel like a city dweller on vacation. Sheilia and I ride in the middle seat of the camper with Rex poking his head out my window. We purchased the puppy at the county pound last summer for Sheilia's seventeenth birthday. "Save a life," she pleaded. "Give me a puppy from the animal shelter for my birthday present."

Three months later Rex ran into the path of an oncoming car and suffered a fractured hip. Sheilia begged her dad to try to save her injured pet. "I'll pay you back no matter what the vet charges," she wept. She did, too, from her paychecks on her job at the National Bureau of Standards. Rex recovered with scarcely a limp. Later, when the girls and I were healing from our own fractures, Sheilia petted her puppy and said, "Rex, we're just like you now."

During the night as we drove through Tennessee the nightmares returned. . . . . *Two ambulances—what are they doing in our lane?* I fought the terror that constricted my throat until I broke loose screaming, "No! No! Not again!"

Rex was barking and Sheilia was shaking me. "Wake up, Mom, everything's okay." She sounded far away.

"There were two ambulances. . . ."

"There were NO ambulances," Tanya interrupted. "You were dreaming."

Fully awake now I sit up and offer Sheilia the chance to stretch out and sleep on the middle seat. We trade places and I sit in the single seat facing the back seat. The brisk night air blowing through the window massages my face.

Why were there two ambulances? The newspapers said there were four called to our accident in Maryland. Is there to be another accident? Lord, help us.

Driving on through Arkansas we arrive Sunday evening at McAlester, Oklahoma. The girls and I look up at Granny's room above the lower level garage. She used to wave to us through the middle window where she peddled her treadle sewing machine making clothes for her great-grandchildren.

Mother and Daddy hurry down the front porch steps holding on to the black wrought iron bannister, Mother in the lead. "I thought I would never see you alive again," she cries as she hugs me carefully.

Daddy's hair has turned gray since I saw him last fall. It's good to have you home, Baby, he smiles with his sad brown eyes. "You too baby girls," he grins as Tanya and Sheilia hug him at the the same time. Yes, it's good to be home again in the town where I grew up and where Richard and I were married.

Bob carries in the overnight bags while Sheilia takes Rex around to the fenced-in back yard. I phone Richard to let him know that we have arrived safely. After supper we talk late into the night with Mother and Daddy. The next morning Aunt Ruth drives up in her white Lincoln town car. She comes in wearing her close-fitting western outfit and her summer Stetson. The girls rush her. "Aunt Ruth, we need to take Bob to the Ken Lance Sports Arena. He's never met Uncle Ken." It's agreed they will go after lunch.

While they're getting their stuff together I lie down on the divan. Mother sits in her rocker smiling. "I can't believe you're actually here. I have to keep looking at you to believe it."

As I close my tired eyes I hear Sheilia tiptoeing past me. "Grandmother, do you need this cover?" She picks up the lightweight summer blanket folded on a chair. When Mother shakes her head Sheilia drapes the soft covering over me. "I thought the air conditioning might be too cool for you, Mom, while you sleep." Her thoughtfulness warms my heart as the blanket warms my aching body. Tears stream down Mother's cheeks.

When Bob and the girls return the next morning Sheilia retrieves Rex from the backyard and we bid a tearful good-by to Mother and Daddy as we leave for Broken Arrow to see Joan and Olan. No sooner do we arrive at Joan's than Richard phones.

"The judge released all witnesses today from the rules of sequestering. Closing arguments will be presented tomorrow and you can be here."

"What? I don't have anything to wear. There isn't time. I'll have to fly."

"You have a reservation in one hour out of Tulsa. The ticket is waiting for you at the American Airlines counter. I bought a blue outfit for you and shoes, too." Richard has good taste in clothes and wisely chose my favorite color. He never mistakes my size either.

"One hour? Sheilia, call your Proctor grandparents in Tulsa. We will need them to take you on to Stillwater and to check you into the dorm. Bob, you and Tanya drive back to Maryland at your own pace. Oh, Joan, please take care of my children again."
Everyone was crying.

"I'll drive you to the airport," Olan said. "I know the quickest route since I drive it every day to work. Where's your bag?"

Free at last. Like the Freedom Fanatics in the children's musical at Westminster, I'm free at last from the rules of sequestering. The trial is over. Alleluia! I can talk about it, read about it, and own my feelings–no matter what the verdict is. As the airliner takes off into the cloudy sky–it's always cloudy over

Tulsa—my imagination paints colorful banners waving over a castle high above the storm clouds. Soon enough I will descend into the real world prepared to fight other dragons.

Richard meets my plane at the Baltimore-Washington airport around midnight. We drive back to Easton talking fast. At the motel he scans his notes from the trial for anything he might have omitted telling me. The newspaper articles raise more questions than they answer in my mind. Too soon the night ends but I slept well in those few hours. No more nightmares.

We arrive early Wednesday morning at the court house. For six long hours the closing arguments are hammered into the minds of the jurors. The defense attorney concludes with the words, "It was only an accident. That's all that it was."

ONLY AN ACCIDENT? My children were slaughtered and it was ONLY AN ACCIDENT? When a man drives under the influence of alcohol, his choice was NO ACCIDENT!

The defendant wanted to believe that seven beers didn't affect him. Sure, and I wanted to believe that my two sons and three granddaughters weren't dead either. Wanting it to be so doesn't make it so. He had four hours in which to make his decision to drink and drive. I had only two seconds in which to escape his vehicle according to the accident reconstruction testimony of an expert witness. It wasn't enough time.

Karl Menninger wrote about the consequences of choices in his book *Whatever Happened to Sin?* He states that persons can choose up to a certain point but beyond that point the choice is no longer theirs. They have entered the zone of consequences. Like the skier racing to outdistance an avalanche I tried to escape the inevitable. My moment in time lasted two seconds.

Jury deliberation will begin tomorrow morning. There's no point in our waiting around. We drive back to Pennsylvania. Thursday, aimlessly making my way between piles of wrapping papers and half empty boxes I pay scarcely any attention to the objects which I am unpacking. Those boxes marked, "Roger's

Things," remain unopened. The phone rings loudly.

"Guilty," Mr. Hickman says, phoning from the court house in Easton. "The verdict is guilty on all counts."

I run across the street to the classroom building to tell Richard. Standing outside the room where he appears to be engaged in an orientation meeting I draw the attention of the instructor. He motions to Richard to join me. We run back across the street to our apartment to phone our families. The phone is ringing as we unlock the door. Reporters want to know our response.

We agree with the verdict. No, we do not seek a maximum sentence. Our major concern is that others be protected from enduring the senseless tragedy our family has suffered.

We're not surprised to learn that sentencing will be handed down in November in order to allow time for a thorough pre-sentencing investigation. It's not over for the defendant and it's not over for us. In a real sense it will never be over for him or for us. But for Tanya, Sheilia, and me, who have been silenced and isolated by the rules of sequestering and forced to live as though the accident never happened—for us, those "twelve days that never were" have ended.

✧ 13

NO TIME to GRIEVE

"O Lord, Thou hast brought my soul up from the grave;
Thou hast kept me alive, that I should not go down to
the pit."

- Psalm 30:3 KJV

Swimming in the fast moving current of opening day activities at the U.S. Army War college I hide my grief within our quarters to be handled privately. The new class of military officers deserves better than a president and his lady in mourning. The welcoming reception is only a few days away. In the meantime we must unpack china and crystal, hang draperies, fill closets and drawers with our clothing, and store everything else in the basement.

The huge rooms with high ceilings, plank floors, and army regulation-white walls must be decorated quickly to welcome guests. After measuring floor space and wall space we arrange the living room furniture and search through boxes for wall hangings and accessories.

This is our twelfth household move in eighteen years on active duty. I would usually set up the kitchen first and hang curtains in the bed rooms in order to make the children feel at home in their new surroundings. This time however we have no children living with us but we will host visitors, dinner guests, and committees in a few days.

I miss Roger and think how much he would have appreciated the stories of this historic post during the Civil War and afterwards as an Indian Industrial school. He would have felt sad for the Indian girl whose ghost is said to roam our quarters. Roger had grown up visiting historic sites with our family wherever we were stationed. The first time we visited Mount Vernon he was three years old. He wanted to know if "George" knew we were there when we toured George Washington's mansion.

A visit to Mount Vernon, home of George Washington. *Left to right.* Tanya, Michael, Sheilia, Ricky, and Roger sitting on Terry Glen's lap. August, 1970.

In order to handle my fragile emotions at the War College I need time alone. A secluded corner in the living room catches the early morning sun and I know that I have found the perfect spot where I can meditate. There I move the stationary rocker which we had purchased at the PX in Germany for the purpose of rocking our grandchildren. Beside it I place a lamp stand with a lower shelf which will hold my journal, Bible, and cassette player.

The sunbeams lighting up the dark corner call to mind the first song I learned to sing, "Jesus Wants Me for a Sunbeam." Not a raindrop, but a sunbeam. Crying unashamedly I run upstairs and locate a Kenneth Copeland tape of praise hymns and scripture songs which my friend Gail Hammer sent to me after the accident. One of my favorites comes from the Old Testament. "I have called you by name; thou art mine. . . when thou walkest through the fire, thou shalt not be burned." Isaiah 43:1-2, KVJ.

Each morning after Richard leaves for class I go to the sunlit corner and turn on the cassette player. I cry through the scripture songs until my tears subside. Then I take up my steno pad and begin to write on a clean page as I talk to God. What comes down on my page amazes me. I keep writing. When I reach the bottom of the page I find that the conflict with which I started the first paragraph has resolved itself. It's like taking an aspirin and vanquishing the pain. Then I wash my face free of tears and dress for the morning's agenda.

Except for the Navy Shipwreck Party official functions were not scheduled for the first few week-ends in order to allow families to get settled. During this period we accepted few invitations for informal socializing but claimed those few week-ends as our unstructured time to mourn our loved ones. We stopped the clocks. If we felt like eating we ate. If we felt like jogging we jogged. We listened to classical music and slept as long or as little as we needed. When the sun had gone down twice we re-set the clocks. It was Sunday night.

If we had not set aside such blocks of unstructured time in

the beginning we would not have been able to function effectively later. Schedules, agendas, and social obligations allowed me a framework in which to serve and find renewed purpose for my life. Journaling insured a space for my private grief work. Living in quarters which had been gutted by fire during the Civil War and rebuilt to serve future generations also gave me a perspective on living with purpose which honors the dead. Sometimes I walked over to the small cemetery at the back gate of the army post to remind myself that I was not the only mother who grieved her dead children, nor would I be the last.

In my blue spiral notebook words stumbled across the pages each morning that had refused to come together the night before in my dreams. Writing for my eyes only I wrote unencumbered, sometimes ripping out pages like a tiger clawing its way out of a trap. Heaps of wadded paper littered the floor. Usually before the hour was over I had resolved my inner turmoil. But one morning I experienced an attack of vertigo when I rose to walk.

The room would not stop spinning. Slumping to the floor I crawled to the phone and called my friend Pat Hick, wife of the post surgeon Colonel Joe Hick. We had met in Germany where Joe had served as Fifth Corps surgeon when Richard served as Seventh Corps surgeon. Pat came over and took me to the clinic where Joe prescribed some medication for dizziness after taking a medical history and examining me. Both Pat and Joe listened patiently as I told them my sorrows. Just talking seemed to calm the storm churning inside me and the dizziness subsided. When Pat took me home I decided to title a new section in my journal, "The Blessings That Overtake Us."

One evening Joe and Pat invited us to dinner. We discussed the fun times in Germany and laughed about the old joke that army wives returned from Germany with a new baby unless they bought a cuckoo clock upon their arrival. Of course both of us had bought our cuckoo clocks and left birthing to the younger army wives.

Joe had met Roger once at Kelley Barracks and I wished

that Roger were here tonight. I related a dream about Roger I had last month and suddenly I started crying. Richard, Joe, and Pat waited for me to go on. No one tried to finish my sentence and I appreciated their sensitivity. Clearing my throat and wiping my eyes I resumed in mid-sentence the tale of the dream and completed it without further breakdown. It was a healing experience for me. The next morning I titled another section in my journal, "Dreams, Memories, Insights."

After that scrumptious meal at Joe and Pat's I felt like I could start cooking again. The last time I invited anyone to a meal that I cooked after the accident the food was tasteless. The guests were Reverend Ruth Ross and her husband Nels. At the time Sheilia told me I should invite them again at a later date and cook the meal right. So I invited Ruth and Nels to drive up to Carlisle from Westminster for a noonday lunch. When I apologized for the tasteless meal at Clarksburg Ruth remarked, "I don't know what you're talking about. We came that day for the fellowship and I don't remember anything being wrong with the food." She was always so kind. When I received her thank-you note a few days later I placed it in another pocket of my journal marked, "Mementoes, Quotes, and Cards." These notes brightened my spirits on dismal days.

As I studied my calendar of official activities I was painfully aware that for the first time since I was fourteen I would not be working with children. Without Roger I had no interface with the teenagers at Carlisle Barracks. I needed time to adjust. One afternoon I was working on business reports for the Officers' Wives Club in the home of another staff officer's wife. We had hoped to finish before school was out but I heard the school bus coming.

"I can finish my part at home," I said as I jumped up and grabbed an armful of papers and folders. "Thanks for helping me." Running out the back door across the parking lot to my own back door I fumbled for my keys. The brakes of the school bus screeched to an ear-splitting halt. Pressing my face against the door, streaking the window panes with gushing tears, I managed to turn the lock and stumble into the kitchen. My arms went limp and folders crashed to the floor scattering papers everywhere.

At least no one noticed me. No one saw me break down. I would be better prepared next time. I would stand at my own door and watch the school bus unload its passengers each day until I could do so without crying. I could handle what I deliberately chose. It was the unforeseen that broke through my defenses.

Richard and I attended a grief recovery class in Carlisle one evening. The woman sitting next to me held her pen tightly but did not write. A man listened with clenched jaws his eyes blinking forcefully. I wondered what circumstances had brought each person here tonight. It is said that grief shared is grief divided. But there was no sharing nor were any discussion groups planned. Only the speaker lectured. We felt uncomfortable with what he was saying and left early.

We received a booklet published by Compassionate Friends and a book by Rabbi Kusher, *When Bad Things Happen to Good People*. Friends gave us subscriptions to to *Guideposts* and similar devotional magazines. Nothing seemed to help enough. I resisted being pigeonholed into experts' grief recovery plans. I must find my own way.

Then I discovered Viktor Frankl's book, *The Psychology of Meaning*. In one word–"meaning"–he named what I was seeking. My children's lives had to mean something more than statistics, more than my personal loss. Frankl, a German Jewish psychiatrist was imprisoned by Hitler. In the concentrations camps he observed that even the deranged prisoners prayed. From his experiences he theorized a concept of being based on awareness at the conscious, subconscious, and unconscious levels. This awareness occurs in a physical body possessing mental capacity and spiritual energy, interrelated and interacting at every level of consciousness. This concept of the wholeness of being appealed to me as I attempted to reconstruct my world.

Studying theology, philosophy, and psychology I found little comfort. Psalms, poetry, and autobiographies of survivors of tragedy consoled me more. Nevertheless I gained useful knowledge and depth of understanding in studying the works of Viktor Frankl, Carl Jung, Elizabeth Kubler-Ross, Carl Becker, and C.S. Lewis, among others. Finally in my journal I named the category for my tears, "The Thorns That Prick."

My five-section journal was fully equipped now to carry me through each morning's journaling session. The ritual evolved as the journal had done according to my personal needs. First, I listened to scripture music tapes with eyes closed. After a while I turned to the Psalms in my blue Bible that I had studied in the hospital. These prayer songs led me into meditation and conversational prayer with God. When I opened my journal to write, I poured out my heart. Sacred time. Sacred moments. Sacred learnings. By the clock the time lasted one hour. It was enough to carry me through the day.

August 11,1982. Major General and Mrs. Richard D. Lawrence officially welcomed the incoming class of officers to the U.S. Army War College with the Commandant's reception at the Officers' Mess. As class president and his lady, Richard and I took our assigned places in the receiving line to greet fellow students and their wives. The trial of the man who killed our loved ones under the influences of alcohol was scarcely a week behind us. However we presumed that most of the officers of the incoming class who arrived from world wide assignments would not know about our accident.

The student body included also a small number of officers from the air force, navy, and national guard branches of military service as well as a few officers from countries friendly to America. Not all students brought their families. "Geographical bachelors" often drove home on week-ends.

The arrival time for guests at the reception was staggered by the seminar groups to which they had been assigned. Halfway through the evening the receiving line took a fifteen-minute break. We were escorted to a private room where we could sit down, chat informally, and enjoy light refreshments. Mrs. Lawrence and I were glad for that opportunity to share our enthusiasm at greeting the wives whose participation would make this a super year for the families. A special military family curriculum would be offered for the first time and these women's input would help to evaluate the the effectiveness of its content and teaching methods. The rest of the evening flowed quickly after the break and I left with a deeper appreciation for the efficiency with which the military system operates in providing for families while fulfilling its objectives.

On the calendar of events one of the first activities of interest to the wives was the Parade of Homes in October. The class president's living quarters are always listed but I was told that I could close off any private rooms if I chose to do so. However I prepared all the rooms since the basement would suffice to hold any extras I could not reasonably display. Most student families lived in small brick houses built early in the twentieth century. Their floor plans varied only in the number of bedrooms which were always inadequate for large families and too small for teenagers. One or two of these homes were scheduled for the tour, usually those whose occupants had no children or only one or two.

The variety of two-story faculty homes inspired the decorating instinct in everyone. The pride of the tour was the "castle" which had been donated to the War College by the widow of the builder who was killed on a safari in East Africa the next year after he built it for her. This gray stone edifice served as the commandant's quarters with its private apartment and its public rooms in which banquets and the community Christmas party and other festivities were held. While a guide escorted the visitors through each host home calling attention to its special features and historical significance, Mrs. Lawrence invited me and a couple of staff officers' wives to accompany her on the tour.

Brochures described the living quarters and the individual styles in which the current occupants had decorated them. For example ours was labeled, "The Second Library of Carlisle Barracks." Bookshelves even lined the upstairs and downstairs hallways representing a lifetime of collecting published works on many subjects. Richard and I had first met in a bookstore, courted at the library, and sat on the steps of the girls' dorm at Oklahoma City University reading to each other before we decided to marry and share our bookcases.

The brochure stated, "Of particular interest in the hallway (downstairs) are the Bolivian Warrior Gods keeping watch over the books, and the exquisite shield from Ethiopia used in the 1896 Battle of Adowa." These books of course covered the history of military exploits.

On October 9, 10, and 11, the Third Military Family Symposium would be held in Washington, D.C. and several of us would be delegates from the class. The theme, "Partners in Progress," underscored the importance of identifying and solving issues related to the military family which affected the retention and effectiveness of officers and soldiers.

General William Tecumseh Sherman had recognized this significant influence of army wives after the Civil War when he encouraged them to accompany their husbands to the frontier despite the failure of Congress to authorize family benefits. Ironically my opportunity to participate in the Symposium came at a time when my own family had just been decimated. Yet even then I realized how very much the army community had supported us in our time of tragedy.

Upon my return to Carlisle Barracks however I was fatigued and decided not to join Richard and other class members with their wives in New York at the Army-Navy game. I slipped into our quarters unnoticed and did not come out until Richard returned. It was a good week-end for both of us. He came home energized and my alone time had revived my spirits.

With my house in order after the Parade of Homes and my cooking skills regained after an evening with Pat Hick I was ready to host small informal dinners. The dining table would seat eight persons comfortably, ten snugly. We always invited a couple of allied officers as well. I missed Tanya's assistance in the kitchen and her congeniality with guests. When we moved to Germany I wondered why it took me so long to prepare and serve a dinner until Sheilia reminded me that Tanya wasn't there to help. Now I didn't have Sheilia's help either since she was away at college in Oklahoma.

We scanned our calendars for the rest of October and discovered that we had scheduled an informal dinner party on the evening of the Historical Trails of Carlisle Walking Tour. "We'll just have to jog," Richard said seriously.

"Are you kidding? I'll be home cooking."

"Use the crockpot. Dessert and a molded salad can be fixed the day before."

Why not? And so we decided that Richard would jog on ahead, read the historical marker, and relate it to me when I caught up. Then he would jog on to the next marker. In this way we finished the trail in half the time required for a walking tour. Laying aside a handful of brochures I quickly showered and dressed for dinner. Richard helped with the meal preparations and we felt quite rejuvenated when our dinner guests arrived.

"Don't expect me to make a habit of jogging before entertaining guests," I warned my husband. He knew better than to press his luck but he held up the medal we each received for choosing to jog instead of walking.

"A nice keepsake, don't you think?"

Prematurely bereft of our children we had to find healthy ways to adjust our lives to our loss. Otherwise we were at great risk for heart attacks, strokes, or other physical or mental breakdowns. Richard participated in the army physical fitness program and I often jogged with him. He timed his laps around the jogging track

141

but I jogged for endurance. Later I signed up for the women's three-mile fun run and laughingly remarked that the only reason I entered was to make the winners feel better.

Throughout the school year the seminar groups competed with each other in athletic events. In the playoff between the army and the air force seminar teams Richard hit a home run with the bases loaded. Richard said that he stepped up to the plate determined to "hit this one for Roger." Wouldn't Roger have been proud to see his dad hit that homer? He should have been there. I placed Richard's trophy alongside Roger's soccer and basketball trophies awarded in Germany and Terry Glen's baseball trophy awarded in Ethiopia.

Tanya did not move to Carlisle Barracks with us. She stayed in Clarksburg to attend Montgomery Community College in September at nearby Germantown. We went back to Clarksburg whenever we could to paint and fix up the house for sale in the spring. In the meantime Tanya enjoyed a circle of friends in the neighborhood and at the college, and visited us at Carlisle when the War College invited the families on a field trip to Gettysburg.

One day in early November we received a call from the Maryland state's attorney office. The sentencing of the man whose decision to drink and drive killed our children would be pronounced on November 15 at the court house in Easton, Maryland. We circled the date in red and phoned Tanya in Clarksburg. We arranged to meet her and Bob in Easton on the 15th.

✧ 14

THE LAW CANNOT SAVE

"Behold, the Lord's hand is not shortened, that it cannot save;
neither his ear heavy, that it cannot hear."
- Isaiah 59:1 KJV

November 15, 1982. In the pre-dawn hours Richard and I step quietly out the back door and unlock our Mercury station wagon in the small parking lot behind Coren Apartments. Under the street light crystal beads of dew drops sparkle on blades of grass bordering the curb. The brisk night air smells fresh and clean. In a few hours the man whose vehicle crossed into my lane and forever changed our lives will be sentenced. The law does not require our presence nor does it require that we even be notified of the sentencing date. But we require it and we will be there.

Leaving Carlisle we watch the bright orange sun ascend silently coloring the Pennsylvania wooded hills in brilliant hues of red, brown, and yellow. If only the darkness in our heart could be dispersed as quickly and our world colored anew in vibrant hues. For nearly a year we have wrestled with the unknown decision the court will pronounce this morning. What would be a fair sentence for a person convicted of five counts of automobile manslaughter, reckless driving, and driving while impaired by alcohol?

We should be celebrating birthdays this months, not memorializing deaths. Last year I baked birthday cakes for Terry Glen on November 1st, Roger on the 9th, Richard on the 18th, and

Becky on the 27th. The birth of Ruth Ann on the 20th, preceded by Richard's and my wedding anniversary on the 19th, made the entire month of November a blessed one to remember when we sat down at the dining room table last November to eat our Thanksgiving dinner with our grandchildren.

Thankfully this month Lieutenant General Julius Becton and his wife Louise happened to be at the War College on Roger's birthday. The general had been invited to lecture to the students, and Mrs. Becton invited another student wife and myself to lunch at a local restaurant. Our conversation inevitably revolved around Roger and the Becton's son Wesley, who was a few years older than Roger. Both boys had suffered from asthma and I mentioned that Roger outgrew his attacks.

"Roger doesn't have asthma anymore?" asked Mrs. Becton before she suddenly remembered that he had died. "Oh, I'm so sorry." We both reached for a kleenex.

"It's okay. We make the same slip when we talk about him too. No, he never had another asthma attack after we left San Antonio."

"Do you have other living children?" asked Charlotte. I didn't know we had been so successful at keeping our grief private. For a moment I couldn't answer.

"Forgive me," she said as she reached out to touch my hand. "I shouldn't have asked that question."

"Yes, we have two sons in Texas and two daughters in Maryland and Oklahoma." At this point I felt I owed her more of an explanation about Roger. "Do you want to know what happened?" What could she say? She nodded and listened as I poured out our story as briefly as possible.

"When we heard about the accident," Mrs. Becton said, "I told Julius that if anyone could handle it, Richard and Martha could." I appreciated her faith in our ability to cope. This morning on our way to Easton my self restraint was being tested again.

Crossing the Maryland state line Richard interrupts the

silence and raises the question which has been on our minds for months. "What kind of sentence would deter people from drinking and driving?" According to the attorneys tough sentences have little effect on people who have an alcohol problem.

We arrive at the Easton courthouse to find Tanya and Bob waiting. Inside the courthouse we ascend the stairs passing the niche where the girls and I waited to testify last summer. Tanya's and my eyes meet for an unspoken moment and we pause briefly. I tell the others I will meet them in the courtroom but I must stop at the ladies' room for now. Freshening my face with a wet paper towel I look into the mirror and am surprised to recognize the faces of the defendant's mother and a younger woman with her. Standing motionless like wild deer sensing danger all three of us stare at each other uncertain as to how to react. Now is not the time to say anything and so I leave without a word.

A few minutes later the two women resume their places in the courtroom in the front row where they sat throughout the trial. Our party sits a few rows back. The defendant's wife holds their young son on her lap. Court convenes and preliminary statements are made. The defense attorney requests permission for the defendant to speak before he is sentenced and permission is granted.

The young man stands and says that he is sorry for what happened. He says that he wishes he could have died instead of the Proctor children. I'm sure he spoke truthfully. I would have felt the same way in his situation.

The child looks into his mother's face at the sound of his father's voice and speaks softly. The judge hears the child and orders the mother to remove him from the courtroom. This brief glimpse of an innocent child, tragically affected by his father's conviction, leaves its impression on the hearers, especially me. I can't stop feeling what a mother feels. My compassion extends to the defendant's mother who lost her husband last January to a heart attack and may lose her son to a prison term today.

145

The state's attorney requests permission to put Richard on the stand to tell how the tragedy has impacted on our family. The judge recesses the court for ten minutes to permit the attorney to search for a precedent and none is found. A victims' rights law was enacted July 1st permitting a victim to submit an impact statement to the court. Why wasn't I allowed to read aloud the statement which I had submitted at the court's request? The judge anticipates my question and looks straight at me when he informs the people that since the accident occurred *before* the victims' rights law was enacted my written statement will not be taken into consideration. On the other hand a quantity of letters written by family and friends of the defendant are allowed.

Richard whispers, "Let's commit him to the Lord." He gazes out the window at the windblown trees shedding their autumn leaves and remarks, "He'll get six months." I write it down.

The judge says that it's the defendant's employer who should be standing here today with the defendant. He says that the employer was guilty of hosting the Christmas Eve party with alcohol when the employees should have been home with their families. That shocks me. Shift the blame to the employer? As I understood it the employer ordered two beers per worker along with the substantial meal. But the defendant continued to order beers after the party for quite some time.

The judge goes on to say that the defendant doesn't have an alcohol problem according to the pre-sentencing investigation. This was only his first offense.

No, your honor, you are dead wrong. He had the alcohol and we have the problem. His first offense killed five people.

The judge lumps all the convictions together as though only one person had died. Punishment will be six months in jail with work time-release on week days to continue his job and support his family, and community service time-release on week-ends. No alcohol rehabilitation treatment is mandated.

Court is summarily dismissed. It's over. The defendant will

sleep nights in jail and work days in the community. In six months he will return to his home and family. We had refused plea bargaining before the trial because we trusted the court system. Apparently we didn't understand enough about the sentencing options. "We could have gotten a better sentence by plea bargaining," the state's attorney and his assistant commented when they accompanied us into a private room.

Tanya cried. "It's as though my children never lived. Their deaths meant nothing out there." Upon leaving the courthouse Richard and I were approached by reporters waiting for our reaction. A correspondent asked me if justice had been done. I told him I didn't know what justice would have been. The defendant had received mercy and there was something he could do. "On Christmas Eve he became involved in the issue of drunk driving. It is my hope that today he will choose to become involved in the campaign *against* drunk driving."

Tanya and Bob had tried to evade the reporters by slipping out a different door but all doors were covered by the media. When finally confronted before TV cameras she solemnly made one statement. "The sentence was unacceptable."

Outside the courthouse I see the defendant's mother hug the attorney who argued her son's case through the long months of judicial process to get the best possible sentence she could have hoped for. My feelings are bittersweet. I hope her son will seek alcohol abuse rehabilitation voluntarily at some time. A few days later someone sends us a short newspaper clipping stating that he had made a statement for tougher laws.

The sentencing receives scant attention in the newspapers. The national interest in the issue of drunk driving has paled and moved on to other sensational stories. It was becoming painfully clear to me that the law cannot save us from each other or from ourselves. The law can punish the guilty but seldom protects the innocent. The record for law enforcement is dismally poor.

Upon our return to Carlisle Barracks we receive an extra

measure of grace this month from our alma mater, Oklahoma City University. A letter informs Richard that he will be honored with the Distinguished Alumni Award at homecoming. Tanya goes with us and Sheilia waits for us in Oklahoma City at the home of her best friend Char Amend, formerly her classmate in Germany. We find that several attendants from our wedding in 1955 are present at the homecoming banquet and we are pleased to introduce our daughters.

"Tanya and Sheilia have such a peace about them," says Helen Taylor. I suspect that maybe their near death experiences had something to do with that. Richard and I had been attendants in Helen and Jim Taylor's wedding the year prior to their being attendants in our wedding.

Another couple who stood by us through the years since our college days are Charlotte and Ewing Inlow. Our two families spent vacations with each in Texas and in Missouri. Roger and the Inlows' son Robin bonded like brothers. Ewing told us that when Richard phoned about the accident Robin was stunned. Days later he asked his dad, "Why? Why did it have to happen to Roger?" We will be asking that question forever, I fear.

We made a quick trip on down to Texas to visit Ricky, Mike, Janice, and Janice's family at the home of her aunt where they had gathered for Thanksgiving. Heading back to Carlisle via Oklahoma to see our parents in Tulsa and in McAlester we felt blessed to have been able to come home again to those who loved us.

Richard intends to drive straight through the night to Carlisle. Tanya dozes off in the back seat on her favorite pillow which cushions her just right. I try to stay awake talking to Richard in the front seat. About 2:00 a.m. somewhere on the interstate highway in Missouri Richard suddenly jerks the station wagon into the next lane. Within seconds a car whizzes past us in the opposite direction in the lane we just exited.

"I saw the beam of his headlights coming over the hill or I

wouldn't have known he was in my lane," Richard explains.

"Please, Richard. It's another holiday week-end and we need to get off the road." Some nightmares are real and this was one of them. We found a motel at the next town and slept safely until nearly noon. We arrived back at Carlisle Barracks with no further close calls.

When November ended we had passed many milestones. Advent had begun however and now I must prepare for Christmas with my family scattered and five empty stockings packed away never again to be filled.

Is This the Way to Bethlehem?

"Therefore the redeemed of the Lord shall return, and
come with singing unto Zion; and everlasting joy shall
be upon their head: they shall obtain gladness and joy;
and sorrow and mourning shall flee away."
                                        - Isaiah 51:11 KJV

The second week in December Kristy Bair phoned from
Westminster, Maryland. "I thought you might find it difficult to
decorate for Christmas this year. Why don't Alice Kushner (the
church librarian) and I come up and help you?"

How thoughtful of them. Alice had sent me grief recovery
literature published by Compassionate Friends, and Kristy phoned
occasionally to let me know our church family was still praying for
us as Christmas approached. The Council on Ministries had
decided not to do the Journey to Bethlehem pageant this year
because the memory of our accident last Christmas Eve was still
too vivid. I understood but I felt sad .

Our Christmas decorations were stored in the basement
except the nativity set which I kept in a box in our closet. I hadn't
planned to display the stable scene this year. In fact I hadn't even
bought a tree but Kristy offered to help me select one. Therefore I
carefully unwrapped and polished each one of the olive wood
nativity figures with Pledge. As I ran my soft cloth along the wood
grain I felt like I was wiping away Paula's fingerprints. Of course

not, I reminded myself, for I had polished them last April when I finally wrapped them in tissue paper and stacked them in the box. Roger's daffodils had bloomed last Easter like a sign that it was time to remove the nativity set and get on with caring for the living symbols of God's grace such as flowers opening in the spring. But now it was Advent again and I dreaded the weeks of preparation for Christmas.

Kristy and Alice arrived beaming like Santa's elves ready to go to work. Kristy opened her car trunk and took out an old cardboard box. "I confess that I had a special reason for offering to help you select a tree. Remember when you told me about the silver tree your children loved in Ethiopia? Well, my husband's employer found this box in a storage closet he was cleaning out for more space. Behold, it contains an aluminum tree. He gave it to John and I brought it with me to the church last Christmas Eve. After the accident I forgot all about it. Would you like to have it?"

Would I? Why the red, blue, and green balls we hung on our first aluminum tree were still packed in their original cartons in the basement. Few had been broken in our many household moves. We still had the spotlight which shone through its four-color rotating panel to bounce the changing colors off the silver branches. Our children, at their young ages, were enchanted.

Kristy and Alice left shortly after lunch, their mission accomplished. I sat down to compose the following story for Mike and Ricky, Tanya and Sheilia.

The Tale of the Silver Christmas Tree

Once upon a time a soldier and his wife and their six children lived in a large stone home in Africa. Their youngest child was a baby boy whom all the children adored. However he was allergic to evergreen trees like his older brothers.

So the soldier surprised his family with a silver Christmas tree he bought at the PX. The children clapped their hands and

151

helped their mother and father hang red, green, and blue balls on the tree. They put on their best clothes and dressed their baby brother in a tiny red Santa suit. Then they sat in front of the glittering tree and smiled while their father snapped their pictures.

Every year the children loved to decorate their silver tree. None of their friends had one like it. One Christmas after they returned to America one of the children asked if he could take the silver tree to school so all the boys and girls could enjoy it. The whole family agreed. Since the family planned to go to Grandmother's and Granddaddy's for Christmas the teacher promised to take it home with her during the holidays. They could pick it up when they returned. It sounded like a very good plan.

Alas, when the young boy went to his teacher's house to get the silver tree she could not find the box. She asker her husband if he knew where the box was.

"Oh, no!" he exclaimed. "The box was so old that I thought it was filled with crinkled wrapping paper. So I put it out with the trash. The garbage truck carried it away."

The young boy was very sad. The teacher and her husband promised to buy another silver tree for the boy but there were no more to be found. Every year the soldier and his family searched for a silver tree but they never found another one.

In the meantime the little brothers outgrew their allergies and were able to have an evergreen Christmas tree just like other boys and girls. They nearly forgot about the silver tree.

Then one Christmas a man found an old box in a closet in the building where he worked. The employees were throwing away a lot of old things to make room for more important things. No one wanted the old box. Do you know what was inside? That's right. A silver Christmas tree.

The man brought it home to his wife. She gave it to the soldier and his wife even though their children were grown now. They were very happy to phone their grown-up children that a silver Christmas tree had come home to stay.

Is This the Way to Bethlehem?

Now every Christmas when the soldier's children come home for the holidays, the silver tree brings back happy memories of their first silver tree in Ethiopia and of the dear friends who blessed their family with this one to replace the lost silver tree.

Nine-year-old Terry Glen holds his six-week-old baby brother Roger beside the new aluminum Christmas tree in 1967 in Asmara, Ethiopia.

With this boost to my spirits I continued decorating the apartment with wreaths on the doors, fragrant red and green candles on the piano, and festive runners on the side tables. We even sent photo Christmas cards to close friends and relatives. Guests came and went, many still unaware of our suppressed grief. But I was unable to hold back the tears when we heard youth caroling outside our living quarters.

"Honey, we must open our door and listen to them," Richard said as he put his arm around my waist. "They will appreciate it." And so we did. Our neighbors told us later that their hearts went out to us when they realized the youth were stopping to sing at our door. I couldn't help thinking that Roger would have been there singing to impress the girls with his musical talent. At that thought I smiled. Maybe I was learning to let go.

The Christmas cards and letters we received brightened our days until the morning I opened the mail and turned the pages of a magazine to a scotch whiskey advertisement. It offered a toast to everyone who showed what Christmas really meant. I screamed and cried, "No, that is NOT what Christmas is all about! My children are DEAD because someone toasted Christmas with alcohol." The ad filled the page. The tragedy filled my life. We must not let Christmas be wrapped in a shroud. When Richard came home I showed him the ad.

"Our family needs to be together for Christmas," he said. "We're going to Oklahoma."

We phoned our parents and asked if they would have room for all of us to come home for Christmas. When there's room in the heart, there's always room in the home. We phoned Tanya in Maryland, Mike, Janice, and Ricky in Texas, and Sheilia in Oklahoma to make plans with us to visit both sets of grandparents like we did when the children were young. We always spent Christmas Eve in Tulsa with Richard's family and Christmas day in McAlester with my family.

I hurried down to the basement storage to locate some old

Christmas tins and the cookie cutters the children used to cut out sugar cookies–reindeer, Christmas trees, stars, and a camel. All weekend I baked sugar cookies and decorated them with powdered sugar and candied sprinkles the way we used to do. I even dropped some blue food coloring into a small amount of powdered sugar frosting and iced the camels blue in memory of Terry Glen who gave his Grandmother Whitlock blue camels one year.

Just when we thought we were almost ready to leave, the phone rang. It was ABC News in New York. Would Richard agree to be interviewed by Greg Jackson on the late night show, "Last Word," tonight? In New York? If we had not stopped to answer the phone we would have been on our way to Oklahoma on our own "Journey to Bethlehem." We would have escaped the drunk driving issue this Christmas.

"If I can say what I need to say, I'll come," I heard Richard stating his terms. "Look at your tape of my interview last year and you'll know what I mean." Greg Jackson promised to let him have his say.

This wasn't exactly "the way to Bethlehem," but it offered an opportunity to share the account of our tragedy in the hopes of saving others from a similar alcohol-related fate. We notified Tanya that we would be delayed but she already knew since the reporters had phoned our house at Clarksburg to get our phone number from her.

We drove over to Harrisburg to catch the shuttle to New York. It didn't look safe to me and I wished we hadn't agreed to go. Would that strange looking aircraft even lift off the ground and, if it did, would it stay in the air long enough to land safely? Fortunately the flight was completed without incident and a limousine was waiting to take us to our hotel, courtesy of ABC. After we checked in and had dinner at a local restaurant we window shopped for a short time and returned to our hotel to prepare for the late night interview. The limousine returned and took us to the studio.

While Richard was being made up for the cameras a young staff member bought in a large plate of fresh fruit tidbits and placed them on the coffee table in the lounge where I waited. Soon a group of young men arrived. Their friend also would appear on tonight's show but for a different reason. As the man and his friends asked about our accident and expressed deep sympathy for our family I was totally unaware that he was an AIDS victim. We had seen the first announcements of this mysterious disease on TV only last year. In our conversations I soon realized that death, whatever the cause, is the great equalizer among survivors as well as the dying.

When Richard and the other TV guest departed the rest of us grew quiet, our eyes fixed on the TV monitor as commercials flashed on the screen preceding tonight's program. The host, Greg Jackson, kept his promise to Richard. He asked questions which allowed Richard to expand on our philosophy of personal accountability for behavior destructive and life-threatening to others, specifically drunk driving. The face-to-face exchange of questions and comments encouraged a more open style of communication than the long distance interview of last year only days after our tragedy. We returned to our hotel hopeful that tonight's program would save lives.

A few hours later, a taxi arrived at the hotel to drive us to the airport. Landing in Harrisburg, Pennsylvania, we claimed our Mercury station wagon in the parking lot and drove on down to Clarksburg, Maryland, to pick up Tanya. At last we were headed home for Christmas.

When we pulled into the driveway in Tulsa early the next morning at the home where Richard spent most of his childhood, Sheilia ran out to greet us. She had come to her grandparents' home from Oklahoma State University at Stillwater and was helping Grandma bake date pinwheel cookies. "My favorite," her dad exclaimed.

"I know," smiled Sheilia. "Mom has the recipe too."

Is This the Way to Bethlehem?

Michael, Janice, and Ricky drove in about noon. Just like last year when the girls and I dashed over to the Gaithersburg mall to shop on the morning of Christmas Eve, Richard and the kids drove off to last minute sales at Sears. Returning with admonitions of, "don't peek," and "close your eyes," they sneaked their purchases into the bedrooms and whispered behind closed doors. The pile of gifts under the tree grew and grew.

Finally everyone was ready to begin the evening's festivities when Grandma served her traditional oyster stew. After quickly washing the dishes we gathered in the living room and handed out the carol books from which we sang every year, even in Ethiopia. I had remembered to bring them. Richard's bass voice and my soprano led the caroling without musical accompaniment. As we looked around the room at each other's faces, eyes began to glisten and voices faltered but we bravely sang on.

Abruptly Ricky got up and with clenched jaw stalked out the front door. He could control his restlessness no longer. Richard followed him. Our voices continued singing while our hearts were praying for Ricky. A few moments later Richard and Ricky stepped back inside with Richard's arm around Ricky's shoulder giving him an affectionate squeeze. They both joined in the singing and Ricky seemed composed. Smiles spread around the circle. I touched Richard' arm when he sat down beside me on the divan.

"It's Easter," I whispered. He didn't know what I meant but for me the feeling of victory over our loved ones' deaths which I had hoped for ever since last Easter was now happening. I leaned over and told Tanya, "It's Easter," and she smiled. She understood.

The grandmother clock on the dining room wall chimed four. Tanya pointed to the clock and said softly, "Mom, we just passed the moment when the accident happened." She paused and added, "This time no one died."

Being here in this house, in the very room where Richard's family first heard the tragic news of our accident, helped me to realize how very much his family and mine had suffered.

157

Our journey back to Bethlehem from Golgotha had taken us through twelve months of soul searching amid rigorous schedules that allowed precious little time to reconcile ourselves to our loss. But today we had successfully gathered three generations of our family in this home to restore Christmas to its rightful place in our hearts. Tomorrow we would do the same with my family at McAlester. Christmas had become Christmas once more.

"And suddenly there was with the angel a multitude of the heavenly host praising God, and saying, Glory to God in the highest, and on earth peace, good will toward men." Luke 2:13-14. KJV.

Colonel Richard O. Proctor and Martha June Proctor December, 1982.

Appendix I

Journaling Through Grief

Select a 5-category spiral notebook in your favorite color with pocket dividers. Label each category as follows:

1. **Daily Log** - Date each entry. Need not be complete.

2. **The Thorns That Prick** - Note those moments that evoke your feelings of emotional and physical pain such as rage, fear, embarrassment, anxiety, sobbing.

3. **The Blessings That Overwhelm Us** - Record the unexpected kindnesses from any source such as a friend or stranger, a change in the weather, or lost items found.

4. **Dreams, Memories, Insights** - Accept your dreams as gifts and examine them for their significance to you. Treasure the pleasant memories. Examine the unpleasant recollections. Forgive. Insights will come when you least expect them. Jot them down.

5. **Mementoes, Quotes, Cards** - Use the pocket for special notes and cards. Record phrases which uplift your spirits. This is your connection with the world beyond your personal loss where wounded healers offer you hope from their own experience.

A special time and place will structure your private time for journaling. Once you start to write you may find yourself jumping from one category to another and back again. So be it. Give yourself permission to feel, to express your thoughts, to scratch out lines or tear out pages. It's your journal, your life, your recovery.

Appendix II

Seven tips for Persons Who Share the Grief

The most comforting ways in which friends shared my grief usually happened without forethought. At other times they resulted from a kind gesture or sensitive comment. I found the following ways to be the most helpful.

1. Allow me to complete my sentences. No matter how awkward the silence between my words may seem to you, it may be a necessary crutch for me.

2. Share your memories of my loved ones with me. Their photographs, letters, and cards sent to you confirm that their lives were meaningful to others.

3. Cry with me. Laugh with me. You need not be strong for me.

4. Touch me. A hug, a steady hand on the shoulder, a soft pat on the arm are reassuring.

5. Invite me out for lunch, shopping, a movie, or a play.

6. Call or visit on special anniversaries such as birthdays of my loved ones. Since I lost children Mother's Day has been my most difficult holiday to endure.

7. Allow *me* to comfort *you* when tragedy comes your way.

The Night the Angels Cried: A Mother's True Story
Order Form

Use this convenient order form to order additional copies of
The Night the Angels Cried: A Mother's True Story

Please Print:

Name_____

Address_____

City_____ **State**_____

Zip_____

Phone(**)**_____

_____ copies of book @ $9.95 each $ _____
Postage and handling @ $2.00 per book $ _____
TX residents add 8.25% tax $ _____
Total amount enclosed $ _____

Make checks payable to June Proctor

Send to June Proctor
RR 4, Box 1193 • Paris, TX 75462